VASARI'S LIFE AND LIVES

Giorgio Vasari: self-portrait (Uffizi).

VASARI'S
LIFE AND LIVES

THE FIRST ART HISTORIAN

EINAR RUD

80 illustrations

D. VAN NOSTRAND COMPANY, INC.

Princeton, New Jersey

TORONTO · NEW YORK · LONDON

Translated from the Danish
'Giorgio Vasari, Renaissancens Kunsthistoriker' by Reginald Spink
Gyldendalske Boghandel, Nordisk Forlag A s, Copenhagen © 1961
This edition © 1963 by Thames and Hudson Limited, London
Printed in Great Britain by Western Printing Services Ltd

Contents

Preface   11

1   An Evening at the Cardinal's   15

2   'Learn diligently, little kinsman'   25

3   Fame and Fortune   70

4   'The Most Eminent Painters . . .'   89

5   Vasari's Sources and Material   129

6   The Style and the Man   151

7   'Accept my work in good part'   166

Bibliography   175

Index   179

Illustrations

Plates in half-tone

Giorgio Vasari: self-portrait. Uffizi Gallery, Florence   *frontis.*

1–2 First and second editions (1550 and 1568) of Vasari's *Lives of the Most Excellent Painters* . . .   p. 17

3 Arezzo: the Piazza Grande. Drawing by André Durand, *c.* 1858   18

4 The Casa Vasari, Via di S. Vito (now Via XX Settembre), Arezzo   18

5 Vasari: painted ceiling in the great hall of the Casa Vasari   35

6 Great hall of the Casa Vasari   35

7 Rome in 1549. Woodcut by Sebastian Münster   36

8 Florence, about 1490. Woodcut by A. Mori and G. Boffito   36

9 Vasari: portrait of his parents. Badia, Arezzo   45

10 Vasari: portrait of his great-grandfather and grandfather. Badia, Arezzo   45

11 Vasari: portrait of his wife, Nicolosa di Francesco Bacci. Casa Vasari, Arezzo   45

12 Vasari: Nicolosa and Giorgio Vasari as SS. Maddalena and Lazzaro. Badia, Arezzo   46

13 Pontormo: Duke Cosimo the Younger. Palazzo Vecchio, Florence   46

14 Raphael: Bindo Altoviti   47

15 Sebastiano del Piombo: Pope Clement VII   47

16 Titian: Cardinal Alessandro Farnese (detail)   47

17 Titian: Cardinal Ippolito de' Medici   p. 47

18 Paolo Giovio. Woodcut by an unknown artist in *Paulus Iovius:
   Elogie Virorum Illustrium* (Basle, 1577)   48

19 Don Vincenzo Borghini. Copper engraving by A. Benaglia in
   Discorsi de V. Borghini (1584)   48

20 Pietro Aretino. Copper engraving by W. Hollar after a portrait
   by Titian   48

21 Benvenuto Cellini. Copper engraving by Samuele Jesi after
   portrait by Vasari   48

22 Vasari: Lorenzo the Magnificent. Uffizi, Florence   65

23 Vasari: Justice. Museo Nazionale, Naples   66

24 Vasari: Scenes from the life of Pope Paul III. Fresco in the Cancelleria, Rome   67

25 Vasari: Scenes from the history of Florence. Frescoes in the
   Palazzo Vecchio, Florence   67

26 Vasari: Pope Leo X and the College of Cardinals. Fresco in the
   Palazzo Vecchio, Florence   68

27 Vasari: Pope Clement VII and the Emperor Charles V. Fresco
   in the Palazzo Vecchio, Florence   68

28 Simone Martini: The Queen of Heaven (La Maestà). Fresco in
   the Palazzo Pubblico, Siena   77

29 Cimabue: Virgin and Child, with angels and St Francis.
   Fresco in the Lower Church of St Francis, Assisi   77

30 Vasari: the Uffizi, Florence   78

31 Vasari, Vignola and Ammannati: the Villa Giulia, Rome   95

32 Vasari: Church of Santo Stefano, Pisa   95

33 Vasari: Palazzo dei Cavalieri, Pisa   95

34 Giotto: Virgin and Child with angels. Uffizi, Florence   96

35 Pietro Lorenzetti: Virgin and Child, with St Francis and St John
   the Evangelist. Fresco in the Lower Church of St Francis, Assisi   105

36   Duccio: Virgin and Child. Detail from the painting 'La Maestà', in the Cathedral Museum, Siena   p. 105

37   Ambrogio Lorenzetti: Detail from 'Good and Bad Government'. Fresco in the Palazzo Pubblico, Siena   106

38   Giotto: Death of St Francis. Fresco in the Bardi Chapel, Santa Croce, Florence   106

39   Masaccio: The Apostles Peter and John giving alms. Fresco in the Brancacci Chapel, Santa Maria del Carmine, Florence   107

40   Fra Angelico: Detail from the 'Crucifixion'. Fresco in the Monastery of San Marco, Florence   108

41   Filippo Lippi: Virgin and Child. Uffizi, Florence   108

42   Piero della Francesca: The Queen of Sheba worshipping the Tree of the Cross. Detail of 'Legend of the Cross'. Fresco in the Church of St Francis, Arezzo   117

43   Andrea Mantegna: Ludovico Gonzaga and his Family. Fresco in the Palazzo Ducale, Mantua   117

44   Luca Signorelli: The Damned. Detail from fresco in the Cathedral, Orvieto   118

45   Botticelli: Birth of Venus. Uffizi, Florence   118

46   Iacopo Pontormo: Resurrection. Fresco in the monastery of the Certosa, Val d'Ema   135

47   Andrea del Sarto: Birth of the Virgin. Fresco in the Church of the Santissima Annunziata, Florence   135

48   Raphael: The Prophet Isaiah. Church of S. Agostino, Rome   136

49   Leonardo da Vinci: St Anne. Detail from 'St Ann with Virgin and Child'. Louvre, Paris   145

50   Michelangelo: The Delphic Sybil. Fresco. Detail from ceiling of the Sistine Chapel, Rome   145

51   Correggio: The Virgin and Child with St Jerome. Pinacoteca, Parma   146

52 Giovanni Bellini: The Dead Christ with His Mother and St John. Brera Museum, Milan   p. 146

53 Giorgione: The Three Philosophers. Kunsthistorisches Museum, Vienna   147

54 Titian: The Venus of Urbino. Uffizi, Florence   147

55 Sebastiano del Piombo: Andrea Doria. Palazzo Doria, Rome   148

56 Andrea del Sarto: Lucrezia del Fede. Prado, Madrid   148

The following portraits of artists in the text are reproduced from woodcuts by Cristofano Coriolani after drawings by Vasari and others in the second (1568) edition of the 'Lives':

1–2 Giotto, Giovanni Cimabue   p. 39

3–4 Simone Martini, Ambrogio Lorenzetti   93

5–6 Piero della Francesca, Masaccio   99

7–8 Fra Angelico, Filippo Lippi   101

9–10 Luca Signorelli, Andrea del Castagno   103

11–12 Raphael, Andrea del Sarto   111

13–14 Botticelli, Iacopo Pontormo   113

15–16 Leonardo da Vinci, Giovanni Bellini   115

17–18 Michelangelo, Titian   121

19–20 Sebastiano del Piombo, Giorgione   123

*. . . in servizio sempre degli
amici, e quanto le mie forze potranno, in
comodo ed augmento di queste
nobilissimi arti*

In Fiorenza, Appresso i Giunti, 1568

Preface

It is now about four hundred years since Giorgio Vasari, painter and architect, published his *Lives of the Most Eminent Italian Painters, Sculptors, and Architects . . . from Cimabue to the Present Day . . .*, a work of biography which may be deemed to have laid the foundations of European art history.

Although this excellent writer, who lived through the Italian High Renaissance and was a friend of Michelangelo, Titian and Pietro Aretino, is mentioned and quoted time and again in the literature of art, with appended biographical data, there seems to be no account of his life, art, or in particular his position as a writer on art, in a form which may nowadays be called adequate. In attempting to repair this omission it has been my aim to provide, besides a general account of Vasari's career, social background, personality, and character, a sketch of his personal milieu, training, and work as a painter and architect, and finally to describe from a modern viewpoint his life's work, the *Lives* which have earned him a lasting and outstanding place in the history of art.

Naturally and understandably, much in his material and opinions has failed to survive the test of later research and criticism; yet his work remains astonishingly fresh, while his descriptions make fascinating reading.

In this book my purpose has been to allow Vasari to a large extent to speak for himself. In order to convey an impression of his original biographical material, I have included extracts, short or long, from his own text, chosen with a view to illustrating his ideas about art and artists that have been regarded since his day as important in the history of painting, together with his personal opinion of their works and his assessment –

favourable or unfavourable – of his fellows and forerunners as men. Except for minor adjustments of his period style, the manner is Vasari's own.

Any account of Vasari would be incomplete unless it were supplemented by autobiographical material taken from his correspondence. A wealth of letters written by and to him has been brought to light within recent years and these are now chiefly located in the Vasari Archives at Arezzo. Together with previously known correspondence they form a collection of over a thousand letters, four hundred of them from his own hand. He corresponded with many of the eminent men of his time: popes, cardinals, princes, as well as gifted critics, scholars, and fellow-artists who were his friends.

Biographies written with a view to publication, and especially auto-biographies, are notable for their modifications and omissions, whereas personal correspondence, expressing moods and emotions of the moment, unedited, lend authentic colour and provide source material about important persons and their correspondents, and in Vasari's case the letters are indispensable as an accompaniment to the rest of the material. Consequently, I have quoted in their context a number of letters, or extracts from letters, translated from the original Italian, which help by their content, style, and tone to illumine his character.

As an architect Vasari was a considerable artist, whose works are still esteemed; yet he regarded himself first and foremost as a painter, indeed an important one, and as a painter he was extremely productive as well as popular, though he seldom rose above the mediocre. His original talent, which is beyond doubt, lacked the opportunity to develop propitiously in the right age, and circumstances forced him to go in for large-scale, indeed factory-produced paintings. In this respect he founded no school, though to some extent he initiated and typified the controversial period in Italian art that is known as Mannerism.

His *Lives* are another matter. He was deeply interested in the history of art from his early youth and he possessed a talent for writing which he was able to develop independently of his other work in the service of art. Furthermore, he received valuable assistance, during the whole course of the work, from some of the most distinguished scholars and authors of his time. They were tireless in their efforts to supply him with information; they provided him with ideas and inspiration, and supervised the technical editing of the vast mass of material; and finally some of them served as 'censors' before the completed work went to press.

As befitted the modern production that it was meant to be, Vasari furnished his book with a large number of portraits of the artists described, done as reliably as the conditions allowed. Some of these portraits (the first series of their kind in literature) are reproduced in this book, along with other material illustrating Vasari and his times, from the original prints in the definitive 1568 edition of the *Lives*, the painters chosen being again those whose work still commands interest today.

While Vasari's work embraces many sculptors, architects, goldsmiths, engravers, and other artists, it has been thought necessary to limit this book to the painters, who indeed were the ones nearest to his heart. For the bulk of the material, with corrections and commentaries, the reader is referred to the standard editions.

I hope that by this means I shall succeed in presenting a vivid as well as authentic picture of Giorgio Vasari, or at any rate a true sketch of him, while at the same time illuminating other prominent persons of the time in the setting of the Renaissance, a period when a new culture throve alongside the unsentimental outlook of the period, with its unrest, its wars, and its plagues.

An account such as this cannot help but touch on matters which fall within the scope of art-historical scholarship and aesthetics, and in this respect I must crave indulgence from the specialists. I may appropriately conclude this foreword by quoting Vasari's own plea to his colleagues, 'The Artists': '. . . do not expect of me what I do not know and cannot perform, being assured of my good intention, which is and always will be to give benefit and pleasure to others.'

I owe thanks to persons and institutions who have afforded me valuable assistance in the preparation of this book, notably Mrs Dyveke Helsted, curator at the Thorvaldsen Museum, and Mr Aage Marcus, author and librarian of the Royal Academy of Fine Arts in Copenhagen, both of whom read the manuscript and gave advice and suggestions. Professor Alessandro del Vita, for many years curator of the Archivio at Arezzo, furnished me with much useful material, and La Soprintendenza alle Gallerie in Florence procured a number of photographs, together with the permission to reproduce them. In conclusion, I wish to thank the staff of the Prints Department of the State Museum of Art, in Copenhagen; Copenhagen libraries, especially the Royal Library, the Library of the Academy of Fine Arts, and the University Library; and—not least—the Dante Alighieri Society of Copenhagen, and other friends who have made it possible to provide the wealth of illustrations.

E. R.

CHAPTER I

An Evening at the Cardinal's

IT WAS a spring evening in Rome. Candles glimmered from the windows of one of the fashionable houses and torch-bearers lighted the entrance for the arriving guests. They were a party of scholars and connoisseurs of art, some in black velvet with silk cloaks, others dressed in brocade with claret and dark-green as the prevailing colours, others again in the violet cloaks of prelates. The men were meeting, as often before, at the Casa Farnese, in order to 'see the Cardinal dine'. After the dinner there was lively conversation – not about politics or Church affairs, but chiefly about the fine arts. The celebrated historian, Paolo Giovio, also famed as the owner of an exquisite art collection, remarked: 'I have always desired to add to my museum a treatise upon the famous masters of art from Cimabue to our own day. . . ' He went on to explain his desire, though with much uncertainty and inaccurate data; whereupon the Cardinal – it was Alessandro Farnese – observed: 'What do you say, Giorgio, would not this be a fine work?'

The eyes of the company were turned on the person to whom the remark had been addressed, a young man in a black cloak, with intelligent eyes and a large, full beard – the thirty-two-year-old painter and architect, Giorgio Vasari.

'Yes, fine, Monsignore, if someone of our profession would assist Monsignore Giovio, in order to put things straight for him and ensure correctness. And I say this because, though he spoke admirably, he confused a good many things.'

'Then give him a list and systematic notes of those artists and their works in chronological order,' said the Cardinal, 'and in so doing render your service to art itself.'

'Selecting what I thought suitable,' Vasari says in his autobiography, 'I took it to Giovio. After praising freely what I had done, he said: "My dear Giorgio, I wish you would undertake this task, and carry it out, for I see you can do it admirably, judging from the specimen which you have given me." '

When Vasari modestly declined, Giovio, supported by the entire company, pressed him persuasively. 'Accordingly I undertook to do so to the best of my powers,' Vasari writes, 'while realizing that it exceeded my ability.'

The scene described took place in the year 1543, under the pontificate of Paul III, when the city was flourishing anew after years of war, disaster, plague and poverty. Scarcely any of those present can have guessed that the work which was there conceived would lay the foundations of modern art history and live on in European literature for four hundred years. It was one of the happy accidents of history – or *was* it an accident? The constellation was extremely favourable: an influential art-collecting historian, at a ripe moment, throws out an idea; it is accepted by an artist exceptionally well read and proficient as a writer, whose ideas about art far exceed the composition of a private catalogue. Probably no other man of his time was so well equipped for the task as he, who, trained as a painter and architect, was familiar with every technical detail of drawing, fresco, tempera and oil, and had also learnt the art of gold-beating. He had a thorough knowledge of marble and other stones, and all the materials of architecture. He was moreover of an age when deliberation does not deter an ambitious man from an imponderable task. Finally, he had long been a passionate collector of drawings by outstanding past and contemporary artists, and of all the information about their lives and work which he could lay hands on. (In his *Libro dei disegni* he possessed drawings by nearly all the artists he mentions in his work, from Cimabue and Giotto. After his death the collection was scattered, but a large proportion ended up in the Uffizi.)

After seven years of labour Vasari's literary life-work duly appeared in 1550. He had put the last words on paper in the summer of 1547, and

1–2 'Lives of the Most Excellent Painters . . .' First edition (above) and second edition.

3 *Arezzo: the Piazza Grande. On the right is the Palazzo alle Colonne.*

4 *The Casa Vasari, now the Vasari Museum at Arezzo. Vasari bought the house half-built at the height of his fame, and decorated it inside and out with his own hands.*

for the fair copy an abbot among his friends made available a monk who was known both for his accuracy in reading handwriting and for his calligraphy. The finished manuscript was sent for inspection by the 'censors', the book's sponsors: the cardinal's secretary Annibale Caro, the poet and humanist Francesco Molza, and the learned theologians Don Miniato Pitti, Don Vincenzo Borghini and Monsignore Giovio – all among the leading names in art, history, and literature, and all eager to give advice and suggestions.

After careful consideration the book was entitled: LE VITE DE' PIÙ ECCELLENTI ARCHITETTI, PITTORI ET SCULTORI ITALIANI DA CIMABUE INSINO A' TEMPI NOSTRI: *Descritte in Lingua Toscana da* M. GIORGIO VASARI, *Pittore Aretino; con una sua utile & necessaria introduzzione a le arti loro.* (The lives of the most eminent Italian architects, painters, and sculptors from Cimabue to the present day, described in the Tuscan language by Giorgio Vasari, painter of Arezzo; together with his useful and necessary introduction to their art.) *plates 1, 2 p. 18*

Published in two octavo volumes, it was printed by Lorenzo Torrentino, the ducal printer, in handsome Renaissance Roman and italic, in 1,036 pages that were embellished with initial vignettes, head-pieces, and tail-pieces in woodcut, representing floral ornaments, birds and biblical figures. The work had four indexes: an introductory list of chapters, a list of the artists individually treated, another of those dealt with summarily, and an index of places where the works mentioned could be seen. As was right and proper, the book was dedicated to Cosimo de' Medici, Duke of Florence, later Grand Duke of Tuscany, who had displayed warm interest in it throughout.

In this work Vasari had erected a Renaissance monument to Italian art over a period of three hundred years down to his own day, and one which was to provide a treasure-house for students of art in after years. The book contained the biographies of some 175 artists; a descriptive list of their work, with information about its whereabouts and subsequent history; and an account of the artists' origins, masters and disciples.

New departure as it was, the work was received with the liveliest interest by the public, and soon it was impossible to procure copies of it even at a high price. But there were those who criticized it from the start, saying that it was too loosely put together; that there were important omissions; that many details were incorrect. Vasari, surprised by his success, himself acknowledged the defects; writing to the Duke of 'this first, sketch-like book', he admitted the justice of some of the criticism and set to work on a revised second edition.

This, the final form of the work, corrected and richly supplemented, appeared eighteen years later as a three-volume quarto edition, produced by the brothers Iacopo and Filippo Giunti at Florence. It now contained 250 biographies and – something of a sensation – included portraits of many of the artists discussed. These pictures were made from drawings by Vasari and his assistants after prototypes which were procured, from many parts of Italy, with the help of artist colleagues, literary friends, and the Duke. They were woodcuts done by one of the best exponents of the technique, Maestro Cristofano Coriolano of Venice. Of bold and handsome line, they are framed by an oval and enclosed by an allegorical decoration in which the three arts are personified.

Later editions, when the blocks were worn out, reproduced the portraits as engravings or lithographs; but none of the later pictures compares with the woodcuts for clarity and faithfulness. Of the likenesses Vasari himself admits that they are – in the case of the oldest – problematical. Artists were not considered worthy subjects of portraiture in the thirteenth and fourteenth centuries. Vasari and his assistants had to pick out in old paintings faces which, according to tradition or written information, represented such-and-such an artist, who had posed for one of the subsidiary figures – a prophet, say, or a warrior, or merely one of a group of peasants.

The years following publication of the expanded and revised work proved that the underlying idea was right and the copious material exactly what the reading public thirsted after. This is borne out by the many editions which succeeded it. In Italy the book was reprinted and published in Bologna in 1647–48 by Carlo Manolessi, with numerous notes and emendations, and embellished as before with the original woodcut portraits, the blocks having been collected by the publisher at great trouble and expense over a period of seven years. Some, however, were so worn that Manolesi had to leave their places open. In 1759–60 came the Rome edition, afterwards highly praised, of Giovanni Bottari, with further notes and critical comments.

In the following centuries numerous more or less complete new editions of Vasari's work appeared; the first to be based on modern principles of research was published in 1878–85, with valuable new, critically treated material, by Gaëtano Milanesi of Florence. This, the twelfth Italian edition, is regarded by most experts as the most valuable down to our day, and forms the basis of most recent Vasari studies. Between 1930 and 1938 Pio Pecchiai published a three-volume edition of the newly annotated biographies, including extracts of letters to and from Vasari, drafts and documents, and much pictorial material illustrating both Vasari's own works and those of artists whom he discussed.

Translations of the *Lives* have appeared over the centuries, the first – in German, by W. Schorn and E. Foerster – in 1832–49, followed in this century by a further German translation, that of Gronau, Gottschewski, and Jaescke, two French translations, three English, and two American editions.

Quotations from Vasari appear in all publications concerning early Italian art, and indeed no writer in this field has been able to dispense with him. We are indebted to him for a vast deal of information which could not have been procured or preserved by any other means: partly because oral transmission came to an end at an early date and the records were lost, and partly because many of the works described have been lost or destroyed. Imitations of Vasari's work were published in his own lifetime, and other writers appropriated his material.

Side by side with the recognition accorded to Vasari's *Lives* in Tuscany when it was published, strong exceptions were taken to it in other parts of Italy, and Federico Zuccari in particular criticized it maliciously. The criticisms were chiefly on two counts. In the first place, Vasari had ascribed the beginnings of the art of painting to Cimabue, though painters had existed in Italy before Cimabue. It can be said in Vasari's defence that all his associates took the same view, and modern scholars are inclined to agree with them that the true art of painting was created, or at least re-created, in Cimabue. The second charge was that he had 'forgotten' or neglected many non-Tuscan artists. This may have been a result of Vasari's fervent patriotism, but there was a livelier interest in the arts, as well as far more favourable conditions of patronage, in Tuscany, and especially Florence, than elsewhere. Finally, it was difficult to obtain adequate information from the other provinces. While Vasari sometimes had difficulty in controlling his private feelings, there is no doubt that he was firmly and honestly convinced of Tuscany's supremacy in Italy and Europe.

A work of such a pioneer character both in approach and in scope was bound to contain a good deal of incorrect information. It became a popular sport, started especially by Manolessi and Bottari, for later editors and adapters to pick holes in Vasari: so much so that those who have taken delight in correcting him appear sometimes to have forgotten or failed to appreciate his great achievement, overlooking the fact that he provided them with such a wealth of material on which to work. Vasari, however, may lie easy in his grave. Even today there is uncertainty and disagreement among scholars with regard to artistic problems and the attribution and dating of many works of art, including some that are credited to the greatest artists.

As a supplement to the *Lives*, Vasari had written a book called *Ragionamenti sopra le Invenzioni da lui dipinti nel Palazzo di Loro Altezze Serenissimi*. . . ('Explanation of the compositions painted by him [Vasari] in Their Serene Highnesses' palace . . .') though it did not appear until 1588, after his death. In form an elaborate dialogue, supposedly between the prince, Don Francesco, and Vasari, the book was intended as a kind of catalogue for public use, enumerating and explaining the many historical and allegorical-mythological compositions which adorned the apartments of the Palazzo Vecchio.

From the *Ragionamenti*, and from scattered statements in the *Lives*, it is possible to glean some idea of the things which Vasari, as well as his Roman-Florentine fellow-painters and the ruling upper class, demanded of painting. He awards pride of place to design, which through the skill of the practised hand governs the rendering of figures in their every pose, turn, and foreshortening, organically linked by grouping. He praises the linear plasticity of Michelangelo and the harmonious group-ings of Raphael, which are in unison with space. According to the requirements of Leonardo and Dürer, figures, buildings, and other objects should epitomize 'the true and beautiful proportions', in which Vasari and his fellows saw elements of the divine. The same applies to the laws of linear perspective as these were formulated by those bril-liant theorists of the fifteenth century, the painters Paolo Uccello and Piero della Francesa and the architect Brunelleschi, and adhered to by every contemporary painter.

Anatomy he regards as extremely important, to be based on long and intensive studies of the nude. Pictorial design is dominated by the studied composition, *l'invenzione*, emphasizing the subject matter, and vitalized by the pose, expression, and gesture of the figures – with strong use of allegorical costume in the monumental pictures, and with symbolical attributes serving to characterize portraits.

Writing of design (*il disegno*) in his introduction to the *Lives* (edition of 1568), Vasari says:

Seeing that design, the parent of our three arts . . ., having its origin in the intellect, draws out from many single things a general judg-ment, it is like a form or idea of all the objects in nature, most mar-vellous in what it compasses, for not only in the bodies of men and of animals but also in plants, in buildings, in sculpture, and in painting, design is cognizant of the proportion of the whole to the parts and of the parts to each other and to the whole. Seeing too that from this knowledge there arises a certain conception and judgment, so that there is formed in the mind that something which afterwards, when expressed by the hands, is called design, we may conclude that design is none other than a visible expression and declaration of our inner conception and of that which others have imagined and given form to in their idea. And from this, perhaps, arose the proverb among the ancients '*ex ungue leonem*' when a certain clever person, seeing carved in a stone block the claw only of a lion, apprehended in his mind from its size and form all the parts of the animal and then the whole together, just as if he had had it present before his eyes. Some believe that accident was the father of design and of the arts, and that use and experience, as foster-mother and schoolmaster, nourished it with the help of knowledge and of reasoning, but I think that, with more truth, accident may be said rather to have given the occasion for design, than to be its father. But let this be as it may. . .

Following Roman-Florentine taste, Vasari requires of colour, especially flesh tints, that it should be true to nature. The traditional medieval preference for the intrinsic colour values, their qualities of harmonizing and contrasting according to established rules, more or less independently of the objects, is abandoned in favour of a representational value which faithfully renders the eye's impression of things seen and yet, as indicated above, is linked to the 'intrinsic design'. He sees modelling as continuous outlines, and shading as variations of the neutral.

While he appreciates the subtle shades of Leonardo and Andrea del Sarto – the Italian *sfumato* – he regards the dissolved outlines and formal creation by painterly means, by colour and tone associated with aerial perspective, in the manner of Titian and the other Venetians, as a breach of accepted style and a decline from it.

Finally, Vasari makes it clear at many points that he greatly esteems the idea of *facilità*, meaning rapidity, ease and deftness of touch, and brilliance of execution with full mastery of technique and control over the materials.

CHAPTER II

'Learn diligently, little kinsman'

GIORGIO VASARI was born on the 30th of July 1511 in the Tuscan town of Arezzo, where his family had a house of their own. Founded as early as the eighth or ninth century B.C., the town was later invaded by the Etruscans, who called it Arretium, and finally conquered by the Romans. Beautifully situated – like all ancient Italian towns – on a range of hills, where four river valleys, among them those of the Arno and Tiber, come together in a rich landscape fruitful in corn and wine, it contained in Vasari's time a large number of antiquities besides purely medieval quarters. In the old churches and palaces were works by distinguished artists like Pietro Lorenzetti and Piero della Francesca. Near by are the beautiful old villages of San Sepolcro, Bibbiena, Poppi, and Lucignano, the hermitage of Camaldoli, and La Verna, the sacred mountain of St Francis. The province of Arezzo still prides itself on having been the birthplace of a number of famous men: the Maecenas of antiquity, the poet Petrarch, and the painters Masaccio, Uccello, Fra Angelico, Piero della Francesca, Luca Signorelli, and Michelangelo.

In this attractive environment Giorgio grew up, the eldest of six children, in a harmonious home with his father Antonio and his mother Maddalena, a home which was afterwards to be hard hit by the plague. The family occupied a respected if humble position in the middle classes. The Vasaris had belonged to Arezzo as far back as was known. Giorgio's great-grandfather Lazzaro was – it is claimed by Vasari – a painter, indeed an admirable artist; but of this loose statement more will be said later. His paternal grandfather, Giorgio the Elder, was a potter, but as described by his grandson a craftsman far

plate 9
p. 45

plate 10
p. 45

above the ordinary. 'He devoted his time continually', Vasari says, 'to antique earthenware vessels of Arezzo, and rediscovered the technique of colouring earthenware in red and black, which had been employed by the Etruscans of Arezzo in the days of King Porsena. Skilful crafts-man that he was, he turned on his potter's wheel large vases a *braccio* and a half high [about three feet], which may still be seen in my house.' One of the four sons, Giorgio's father, continued the pottery-making; another, who also bore the name of Antonio, became a priest and was later a staunch supporter of young Giorgio.

Giorgio's father detected artistic talent in him at an early age, and when the boy was eight or nine began to have him taught drawing. Soon after, an elderly relation of the family, Luca Signorelli, a painter celebrated throughout Italy, came to Arezzo in order to supervise the erection of an altarpiece he had painted for the nuns of the town. He stayed at the Vasaris' house and observed the boy's liking for art. 'Luca turned to my father and said,' Vasari relates, ' "Let Giorgio at all events learn to draw . . . for even though he should return to other studies, the ability to draw would be useful and honourable to him, as to all men of culture." To me, he said: "Learn diligently, little kinsman." ' Some time later, the town was visited by another outstanding artist, Guglielmo da Marcilla (William of Marseilles), a Dominican monk, who in his homeland had achieved the highest fame as a maker of stained glass. Guglielmo, who had been called to Italy by the Pope in order to execute works in the Vatican, and who was generally called 'The Prior', was, Vasari writes later, 'a noble-minded man, richly talented, and greatly experienced in the art of glass. He created perspective in his pictures by different firing of the colours, and he was incredibly skilled in fitting the joints of the lead and in the technique of producing colours.' He settled in Arezzo for the rest of his life. From him Giorgio received his first systematic instruction in painting, and he remembered this teacher with the deepest veneration ever after.

Being in every way precocious, the boy when still young was given an all-round humanistic education by local teachers, notably the poet Giovanni Pollastra of Siena. He was a man of great learning, but doubtless his teaching was marked by the dryness and pedantry that is characteristic of the writings he has left, of which the most important is a life of St Catherine.

Just as intelligent pupils nowadays are helped on by scholarships and free places in schools, in those times the ablest – with a little luck – came under the patronage of some aristocratic benefactor. When he was thirteen Giorgio, a bright star among his fellows, was recommended to the cardinal of Cortona, Silvio Passerini, when he, as papal legate and temporary regent of Florence, broke his journey to that city at Arezzo. Giorgio's father, who was a distant relative of the cardinal, seized the opportunity to procure the desired protection for his son. The outcome of the presentation being favourable, the boy was taken to the capital along with the cardinal's wards of the same age, the two sons of the house of Medici: Alessandro, afterwards Duke of Tuscany, and Ippolito, later cardinal. Both were – until struck down by fate – to be his influential friends and protectors.

In Florence Giorgio, by provision of the cardinal, was lodged in a noble house belonging to Niccolo Vespucci, knight of Rhodes, an upright man who enjoyed general respect among the citizens. The house stood close to the old goldsmiths' bridge, central and extremely convenient for excursions by the inquiring boy. He could walk southward along the Arno to the ducal gardens; from his home it was only a few minutes' walk to the splendid palaces which even then gave the city an air of old and distinguished culture.

plate 8
p. 36

Across the river, then as now, twisting roads led up the 'mountain', which was crowned by an ancient monastery and the venerable Romanesque church dedicated to San Miniato. To the north loomed the heights of Fiesole, and against the eastern and the western horizons picturesque mountains towered in the distant blue mist. A panorama which must have fascinated him Giorgio found in the picture of the city spread out on both banks of the river at the mountain foot, its towers and domes outlined against the sky at sunset.

Giorgio was soon able to continue his humanistic education, as for a period – how long, we do not know – he received instruction for an hour or two each day from the learned Piero Valeriano, along with the two young Medici. Valeriano had spent his life in the study of ancient literature and art and was particularly fascinated by Egyptian hieroglyphs. Believing them to be, not picture writing, but allegories and symbols, he published a voluminous work called *Hieroglyphica*, in which he sought to interpret their mysterious meaning. Vasari no doubt owed his intimate knowledge of the realm of allegory and symbol, which he afterwards widely explored, to Valeriano.

The art of his own time also manifested itself to him; for through the Medici family he was brought into close contact with Michelangelo, whose work he was able to watch, every day for three months, in the new sacristy of the church of San Lorenzo, which was destined to be the resting place of the princely family; in the master's studio – a glorious opportunity! – he witnessed the birth of 'Night', 'Day', and the other sculptures that were to decorate the Medici chapel. Writing later in his book, he says: 'What am I to say of "Night" – a statue not rare but unique? . . . What century before this has seen statues, ancient or modern, displaying not only the sleeper's repose but also the passionate grief felt by her at the loss of something great and noble?'

Michelangelo made an overwhelming impression on Giorgio by his entire personality, and he remained for the rest of his life Giorgio's admired friend and master.

From those early years, when the enemy were in the land and the citizens had risen to expel the Medici from the city, Vasari recalls the following incident:

In 1527, when the excited populace of Florence rose against the Medici, the troops tried to storm the Palazzo Vecchio and the defenders threw a bench from the palace of the Signoria on to those who were attacking the gate. Unfortunately, it struck an arm of Michelangelo's 'David', which is beside the gate, and broke it into three pieces. The pieces had lain there for three days when Francesco de' Rossi (Salviati) called on Giorgio and, children as they were, they went to the piazza and fearlessly picked up the pieces among the guard and took them to the house of Francesco's father. Afterwards Duke Cosimo received the pieces and had them put together with copper rivets.

During the banishment of the Medici, Michelangelo had been one of the 'Nine' who had occupied high office, serving as controller-general of fortifications, and for the rest being able to work only secretly in the sacristy. Because of his activities he had more than once had to flee the city, and when called back to Rome in order to resume his work on the tomb of Pope Julius he left Florence, where peace and quiet had come to an end. Giorgio had to fend for himself. The city was in a desperate situation; under the Prince of Orange, the imperial army had overrun the country after the sack of Rome in 1527, and privation and the plague had followed in its wake. In 1529 the Pope made 'peace' with the emperor – a peace which, as Gregorovius says, meant the political death of Italy. The Prince of Orange encamped with his rabble of Spaniards, Germans, and renegade Italians outside Florence; and through siege, bombardment, starvation, and the inroads of the plague the fate of the city was sealed by capitulation. Though the emperor granted an amnesty, Florence had to submit to the reinstatement of the Medici rulers, in the first instance Alessandro, the emperor's son-in-law.

After the death from the plague in 1527 of Vasari's father, thirteen-year-old brother, and several other members of the household, his uncle, Don Antonio, caused him to be removed from the city, where for a short period he had been apprenticed to the painter Andrea del Sarto and the sculptor Baccio Bandinelli, into the country, until such time as the plague began to subside. 'However,' Vasari says,

> I did not lose heart but returned to Florence. Realizing that it would be some time before I should be able by my painting to keep a brother, my mother, and the three sisters left to me by my father, I apprenticed myself to a goldsmith – though for only a brief period, since on the arrival in Florence in 1529 of the army I accompanied my good friend, the goldsmith Manno, to Pisa. But I soon gave up goldsmith's work for painting.

As the war drew daily nearer, I decided to return to the city of my birth; and being unable to proceed by the usual route, crossed the mountains to Bologna, where preparations were being made for the entry and coronation of Charles v, . . . and so on to Arezzo.

In Bologna, triumphal arches were being erected and preparations were being made for other celebrations, and Giorgio obtained employ-ment in this connection. It was work which proved to be well suited to a man of his abilities, and even the greatest of artists were not above this sort of thing.

So as not to be idle in Arezzo [he goes on], I began painting a little in fresco, though in fact I had never had anything to do with colours before. I found the home in good order, thanks to the care of my uncle; and, my mind at rest, I continued to draw and paint. Then Don Miniato Pitti, prior of an Olivetan monastery in the province of Siena, sent for me, and got me to do some pictures.

When, shortly after, he became abbot of San Bernardo, Arezzo, he commissioned me to do several pictures for his church.

In 1528 Vasari had made the acquaintance of the painter Rosso Fiorentino, who was working at the time in the nearby town of San Sepolcro. This gifted artist encouraged Giorgio by giving him sketches and ideas for pictures, as well as procuring him new commissions.

In 1530, when he was nearly twenty, we find Vasari for the first time in Rome, invited by his patron, Ippolito, who in the meantime had been raised to the rank of cardinal by his uncle the Pope. This youthful benefactor gave him a couple of rooms in his palace as a lodging and allowed him to dine at his pages' table. An agreement entered into with his patron has been found among Vasari's remains: it shows that he was to have three gold *scudi* a month in salary, plus the mentioned emolu-ments. For this he was to work for Ippolito for three days a week. The rest of his time was to be his own, but he was to show the drawings resulting from his studies to the cardinal every morning and evening.

To a traveller the papal city must have seemed empty and sparsely inhabited, except at its central points: the Borgo, with its jumble of

plate 17
p. 47

Vatican buildings, courts, and gardens; the quarter 'By the Bridge';
and the ever-lively district of Trastevere. The Quirinal hill was in those
days virtually a refuse dump, and the Palatine hill, which in the distant
past had been so distinguished, was a veritable jungle. It was only three
years since the ruthless sack of Rome, referred to later by Vasari in these
terms: 'Then God, wishing to punish this city and cast down its arrogance, permitted the Constable Bourbon to invest the city with his
army and for six days plunder and ravage it with fire and sword. . .'
Over half of the inhabitants, numbering originally 65,000, perished
from slaughter, starvation, famine, the plague and other diseases, and
many fled to other parts. Among artists, Baldassare Peruzzi was taken
prisoner and tortured by the Spaniards; Rosso Fiorentino was captured
by the Germans and forced to work as a common labourer; the architect and sculptor Sansovino escaped at great peril to Venice; while
Michelangelo fortunately happened to be away from the city at the
time.

plate 7
p. 36

Yet in the circle of the Pope there was life; a host of scholars and
writers, poets, painters, sculptors, architects and goldsmiths thronged
the Curia; there were swarms of time-servers, soldiers of fortune, and
swindlers. The Pope and the leading prelates devoted much time to
arranging and attending all kinds of entertainment. An Academy had
long existed; active originally in a spirit of Latin humanism, cultivating
literature, languages and rhetoric, after the sack it was mostly recruited
from lyrical poets, improvisers and playwrights, who wrote couplets,
mystery plays, and dramas in the style of Plautus – as a rule extremely
frivolous (some of the worst were by Cardinal Bibbiena), but magnificently presented. Vasari's later friend and literary supporter, Claudio
Tolomei of Siena, had founded in 1530, in association with Paolo
Giovio, and under the patronage of Cardinal Ippolito, a new Academy,
which was named *L'Accademia della Virtù*.

On all occasions, processions and 'triumphs' in ancient style were
held: great public festivals, brilliant with magnificently coloured costumes,
banners, and wagons with tableaux – all enlivened by musicians, acro-
bats and conjurers.

Yet it must be said that the great were also eager to promote true art. The building of St Peter's went on with renewed vigour at this time. The Palazzo Farnese made good progress towards completion, and many other splendid new buildings added lustre to the city. Numerous painters were active alongside the architects, though the original circle had been split up and some of its members had left Rome for good.

Giorgio applied himself with zeal. With his friend Franceso Salviati, he roamed the papal city ceaselessly, looking for antiquities and the art of the past, much of which had miraculously survived the sack.

We worked together all the winter [he writes], drawing from morn-ing to night all we saw – for preference the works of Raphael – often living only on bread, and nearly stiff with cold. Drawing day and night became a habit which I could never afterwards grow out of . . . and I can truthfully say that those opportunities and that study then were my real teachers of this art. . . . In order to have drawings of everything, we each drew different things, and at night each copied the other's work, so as to save time and learn the more, taking our very modest morning meal standing up.

After this incredible labour, the first work to issue from my own workshop, so to speak, was a large picture of life-size figures, a Venus with the Graces adorning themselves. Cardinal Ippolito had commissioned it of me; but I will not dwell on this picture, as it was the work of a young man, and I would not mention it but for the fact that I like to recall those first steps and the many helping hands that supported me.

Giorgio's fee amounted to twenty gold *scudi*.

This gentleman [Ippolito] encouraged me to believe that this picture was by way of being a good beginning, effective and full of life. And as, among other things, I had from my own imagination included an exuberant satyr, hidden in the bushes and gloating over the sight of the naked Graces and Venus, the cardinal was so de-lighted that he had me fitted out with new clothes and desired me to paint another and larger picture, also in oils, of a combat between satyrs, fawns, bacchantes, and cupids, representing a sort of bacchanal.

About this time Ippolito was appointed papal legate to Hungary and he commended Giorgio to the Pope, Clement VII. This worldly prelate, formerly Cardinal Giulio de' Medici, though a vacillating politician was a splendid patron and Giorgio was well received by him. Vasari had now been introduced to the Medici family in earnest, and through the recommendation of the Pope he gained access to Alessandro, the soninlaw of Charles v, who by the Emperor's order had been made Duke of Florence.

plate 15
p. 47

Soon back in that city, Vasari was commissioned to paint a portrait of the Duke in full armour, and the work, finding great favour, led to the commissioning of a larger one: a series of pictures representing the deeds of Caesar for a room in the Palazzo Medici. These he embarked upon with the utmost energy, and they earned him a substantial fee.

At the same time Vasari painted for an uncle of the Medici, Messer Ottaviano de' Medici, an allegorical portrait of Lorenzo the Magnificent, which was probably inspired by Pontormo's portrait of Cosimo the Elder. This picture has since been esteemed for its profound characterization, and is exhibited in the Uffizi alongside Pontormo's. Writing to the Duke, Vasari describes how he painted the 'Lorenzo', 'seated in a long cloak of green material lined with white wolfskin. In a broad antique leather belt hangs a purse of red velvet; the right arm rests on a pillar bearing a head of Falsehood biting its own tongue, partly covered by Il Magnifico's right hand. On the pillar is written: "Like my ancestors before me, so have I shone by my virtue for generations to come." At the side is an ugly mask of Vice bearing a vase, in pure style, on which are inscribed these words: "The vessel of all virtues." '

plate 22
p. 65

The Duke, who according to contemporary accounts had otherwise a poor reputation, made good provision for Vasari, allowing him a regular salary of six gold *scudi* a month, board for himself and a servant, lodging, and other amenities.

During those years Giorgio made many acquaintances who were to be agreeable and profitable to him later on. Besides the Medici and other influential patrons, he met humanist scholars and writers, as well as many fellow-artists. In the *Lives* he recalls with particular affection the painters Iacopo Pontormo and Angelo Bronzino. He says of Pontormo that he was an excellent painter, especially in decoration and portraiture, where he had his own admirable style. Writing of a development in Pontormo's manner of painting that was to have far-reaching significance in the history of art, he says:

In 1522, when the plague broke out in Florence and many people fled in order to escape infection, Iacopo also decided to leave the city. The prior of the Certosa . . . wished to have some fresco paintings at the corners of a large and beautiful cloister surrounding a lawn, and he offered the commission to Iacopo, who readily accepted it. His sole assistant was his pupil Bronzino. While enjoying the quiet and solitude that were so dear to him, Iacopo thought it a good opportunity to show the world that he had attained to an even greater perfection, as also to a style different from that of his other works.

Not long before, a large number of delicate engravings by Albrecht Dürer had arrived in Florence, among them many scenes, both large and small, from the Passion of Christ. They displayed the utmost perfection of engraving, both in beauty, variety of costume, and composition. Having to paint scenes from the Passion himself, Iacopo determined to make use of these *invenzioni* by Dürer, expecting thereby to please both himself and most Florentine artists, who were united in their praise for the beauty and excellence of Dürer's engravings.

Accordingly, Iacopo began to copy this style; and striving to invest the facial expressions of his figures with the same immediacy and variety as Albrecht's, he was so successful in emulating him that the charm of his original style, a gift of Nature, full of sweetness and grace, was so impaired by this new ambition, and by contact with this German style, that, beautiful as these works could be, little of

5 *Ceiling of the main hall in the Casa Vasari.*

6 *Casa Vasari:*
   the main hall.

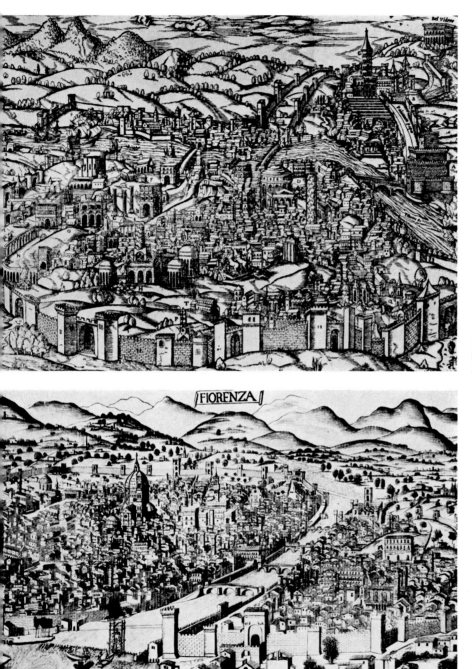

7 Rome in 1549: woodcut by Sebastian Münster.

8 Florence, about 1490: woodcut by Mori and Boffito. The city even then had an air of old and distinguished culture.

the excellence and attractiveness of his former figures are recognizable in them. . . . They invoke in the beholder a feeling of pity for the simplicity of this man Iacopo, who strove with so much patience to learn what others aspire to forget, thereby abandoning the style which excelled every other in delicacy and which gave exceeding pleasure to all. Could Iacopo have been ignorant of the fact that Germans and Flemings come to this country in order to learn the Italian style; which he took such pains to discard, as though it was of no use? . . . When Iacopo eventually came to paint the Resurrection, like a man unfixed in his principles and consequently on the look-out for any-thing new, he had the idea of changing his colouring and painting this work in fresco, in such a manner that had he adopted any other style but the German it would have been marvellously beautiful. . . .

Modern art historians have recognized Pontormo's Certosa frescoes as a radical break with tradition; for in Dürer's works the painter was seeking support and inspiration which were in line with his own psycho-logical approach, as we shall see later on. The work in question is recognized as embodying something that is fundamental to the artistic view of the Late Renaissance, of Mannerism. To his contemporaries, these pictures by Pontormo seemed to be a deplorable lapse from the Italian ideals. *plate 46* *p. 135*

Vasari says that Pontormo afterwards regretted his mistake and sought to approach the style of Michelangelo – a development satisfying to him but regretted by posterity. 'For the rest,' Vasari relates, 'Iacopo earned good money, and despite his unpretentious nature built himself a house, to which he would often retire, some say to the loft, drawing the ladder up behind him and closing the hatch in order to be in peace.' In time he became an odd, hypochondriacal recluse, with a dread of crowds, disease and funeral processions.

A man of an entirely different character was Bronzino, a pupil of Pontormo and afterwards, as court painter, a colleague of Vasari's. 'He was amiable and placid, never doing anyone wrong; welcoming all able men in his profession. I, who have enjoyed close friendship with him for 43 years, from 1524 until the present (1567), can testify to this; for at that time I began to know and appreciate him . . . when he was working under Pontormo. . . . His portraits are all faithful and done with great industry: so perfect that no more could be asked for.' He was the pupil whom Pontormo chose as his assistant when working on the Certosa frescoes, and the one who was most devoted to his exacting master.

We can endorse Vasari's appreciation of the portraits of these masters; those of both, and especially those of Pontormo, are far superior to his own. With the exception of Pontormo's Certosa works and his decorations of Ottaviano's villa at Poggia a Caiano, their 'histories', though interesting, afford little pleasure to a present-day viewer.

After this digression in order to indicate Vasari's position among contemporary painters, let us return to his career.

Vasari's industry and accommodating nature soon gained him a big new commission, comprising the festival arrangements, together with the construction and decoration of the triumphal arches and other preparations, connected with the visit to Florence of the Emperor Charles v. Vasari set to work on the planning and designing of vast platforms, arches and structural decorations, with statues, paintings and inscriptions. He also designed a banner of crimson fabric, thirty feet deep and eighty feet long, gilded with 50,000 small leaves of gold, to fly over the Palazzo Vecchio.

Vasari says of this event:

Unfortunately, it was becoming a widespread opinion in the city that Vasari was too highly favoured by the Duke, compared with other artists and craftsmen. His rivals conspired to embarrass Vasari, and make him a general laughing-stock on the day of the festival. No master mason or carpenter or other young men in the city could be induced to assist him. Vasari, when he became aware of this, sent word for three of his own assistants, in the first place Cristofano Gherardi, called Doceno, and with the help of these and other painters from Arezzo and elsewhere he succeeded in completing the work in time. Cristofano was so outstanding that he astonished

Giotto   Cimabue

everyone, earning for himself and Vasari, who won much praise for these works, both honour and untold glory.

Gherardi, though older than Vasari, was his pupil and close friend, and in time became his most trusted and efficient assistant. 'Cristofano', Vasari says, 'was a droll, amusing, cheerful and excellent painter.' He is the subject of an entertaining story in the *Lives*.

Cristofano was careless outside his craft, so much so that he never wore new clothes. Often he would be in such a hurry in the morning that he would put on odd shoes, and usually he would wear his cloak inside out, with the hood inside. . . . One morning the Duke and Duchess saw him dressed thus, and the Duke asked: 'Cristofano, how is it that you always wear your cloak inside out?' Cristofano replied: 'Sir, I do not know; but I hope one day to find a cloak that has neither inside nor outside, and is alike on both sides . . . but your Excellency should look at what I paint, rather than how I am dressed.'

39

The Duke made no reply, but in the course of a few days he had a cloak made of fine cloth, in which every part was sewn in such a way that it was impossible to tell the outside from the inside, and had it taken to Cristofano. . . . It was a great joke when Vasari secretly took away Cristofano's old clothes and laid new ones out for him, to hear him, as he angrily had to put on the new ones, exclaim: 'What outrage is this? Why cannot a man live as he pleases?'

Though not outstanding, Cristofano was a very useful assistant, being a fast and hard-working painter. He could barely wait of a morning for it to grow light before settling down to work. He was rather indifferent to fees, and it is not to be wondered at that he became Vasari's best helper in the great works to come.

The Duke, highly satisfied with Vasari's festival arrangements, gave him the considerable fee of four hundred gold *scudi*, plus a bonus of three hundred – the payment which the colleagues who had let him down were to have had. These earnings straightened out his economy, enabling him to marry off one of his sisters and place the second one in a convent, both with respectable dowries.

Yet the times were, to say the least, uncertain. 'While I was thus winning honour, fame, and riches,' Vasari says in his autobiography, 'my master Alessandro was cruelly murdered' – in the judgment of history, not undeservedly. A few years earlier, two other patrons of Vasari in the Medici family, Pope Clement VII and Cardinal Ippolito, had died. The latter had succumbed to 'a fever or poison'. A trusted man in his service, the learned jurist Gabriello Cesano, declared under cross-examination that the cardinal had been poisoned, and evil tongues maintained that Alessandro was behind it.

The twenty-six-year-old Giorgio was shocked by the Duke's sudden death. Seeing his future plans thwarted, he was on the verge of despair. His concern and despondency are expressed in a letter which he wrote, the day after the murder, to his uncle, the worthy Don Antonio:

See now, dear uncle, how my hopes in the world and the gifts of fortune, and my reliance on princes, and the rewards of my great

exertions – how they have all ended – blown away by a puff of wind!
See how Duke Alessandro, my master on earth, is dead, killed off
like a wild beast in cruelty and jealousy by Lorenzo di Pier Francesco,
his cousin [Lorenzino de' Medici, later killed at the orders of Duke
Cosimo].

Along with everyone in his service, I mourn his misfortune: that so
many swords, so many weapons, so many mercenaries, so many
sentinels could do nothing against a single sword and two
abandoned, perfidious traitors.

I do not, however, mourn – as many do – *their* misfortune, the
seducers', tricksters', and procurers' (because the court is continuously
nourished by flatteries), if their trade engenders not only their prince's
death but that of everyone who worships the world, mocks God, and
is left in the misery which has tonight overtaken His Excellency and
all his servants.

I confess, in the name of truth, that my arrogance had risen so
high through the favour I enjoyed, first with Cardinal Ippolito, and
then with Clement VII, his uncle, both now snatched away by
death, that I fell from the hope of Church favours for you, who
maintain my house, my mother, my sisters, and my brother, the hope
by which I would one day reward and honour you for your conduct
and perfect goodness to me and my household.

Now, after Death has broken the chains which I had previously
taken upon me in respect of this celebrated house, I have resolved to
absent myself for a time from all courts, ecclesiastical and secular.

Acknowledging by these examples that God will have greater
mercy upon me when He sees me making my way from town to
town, creating adornments for the world by the humble ability He
has given me, I confess His glory and declare my continued readi‑
ness to serve Him. If I am to continue in His service, I think that,
as the Providence He also is for all the birds and beasts of the earth,
He will provide constant work for me to do, in order that, by the
sweat of my brow, I may assist you and all my household, over
and above what I could have done in a service I might have

obtained under Cosimo de' Medici, an elected prince, where I could
have had the same position and salary. . . .

Giorgio seems to have resolved on leaving the city and its agitated
atmosphere, but finding all the gates shut he had to stay. After placing
his valuables in safety, he retired to the monastery of the Servites, where
he had stayed before.

Soon afterwards, he obtained a commission which, at this critical time,
was exactly to his liking: through his old teacher, Giovanni Pollastra, he
was invited to the mountain monastery of Camaldoli, where the monks
planned to have their church decorated in fresco. This old monastery,
founded in the thirteenth century, is picturesquely situated on a slope of
the Apennines amid the magnificent scenery of Casentino, some thirty
miles to the north of Arezzo. The serenity of the holy place and the
solitude of the mountains were balm to Giorgio's heart after the harrow-
ing events in Florence. Soon his sketches were ready; and as these met
with the approval of the fathers of the hermitage, he plunged into the
work during the summer, with the promise and intention of returning
the following summer.

After another, shorter stay in Rome, where he benefited by a letter
of credit for 500 gold *scudi*, given to him by his client and afterwards good
friend, Ottaviano de' Medici, for the purpose of study, Giorgio was
able to execute some works which won him respect as a painter. His
friend Miniato Pitti had recommended him to the abbot of the monastery of S. Michele in Bosco, near Bologna. There he did a decoration
in fresco and oils, a scene from which, showing Christ with Martha
and Mary, is still at the same place; another, representing the feast of St
Gregory, in which he adroitly portrayed a number of prominent persons
– among them Pope Clement as Gregory – is in the Pinacoteca at
Bologna. These works, influenced by the Roman style, displayed
considerable skill and originality.

The year after, when Vasari was painting away in fine form for the
devout and friendly Camaldolensi, good fortune again came to his aid.
Staying in the remote and wooded region that summer was a man of

uncommon influence, Messer Bindo Altoviti. He was one of the country's great merchants, Florentine consul in Rome, and banker for the Curia. He possessed considerable humanistic culture and was a great art-lover (Raphael had painted his portrait as a young man). He had come to Casentino on behalf of the Pope in order to arrange for the purchase and transport of large quantities of deal for use in the construction of St Peter's. On his local excursions he visited Camaldoli and there saw Vasari's works, was attracted by them, and commissioned him to do an altarpiece for his church in Florence. This earned for Vasari, in addition to the respectable sum of 300 gold *scudi*, the warm friendship of Bindo and a standing invitation to stay at his house in Rome whenever he pleased. This house, richly furnished and filled with precious things, was near the Ponte di S. Angelo, a central quarter where the other great banking houses of Tornabuoni, Pazzi and Fugger also had their offices.

plate 14
p. 47

After his temporary revulsion from service at court, Vasari could not resist an engagement now by Duke Cosimo, who needed him in the construction of his fortifications at Florence.

In Rome, whenever there was an opportunity, Giorgio had taken up in his spare time his old passion of drawing; striving with all his energies to make up for lost time during his first stay, he possessed 'before long', he says, 'over three hundred drawings'. Bindo esteemed him so highly that he suggested he should settle permanently in Rome in order to paint for him; and together with Paolo Giovio, who had an influential position at the Curia ('that apostolic parasite', as their sharp-tongued friend Pietro Aretino called him), he began to prepare for his entry into the highest papal circles.

plate 18
p. 48

Meanwhile, Vasari had felt an irresistible urge to visit Venice, whither he had been invited by Aretino, 'the celebrated poet and my firm friend, who greatly desired to see me. I was glad to do so in order to see the pictures of Titian and other painters; which indeed I succeeded in doing, seeing in the course of a few days the works of Correggio at Modena and Parma, and those of Giulio Romano at Mantua.'

Perhaps he feared or suspected that the school of painting which had arisen in Venice and its surroundings, and which was already well known, held something new for his homeland, and threatened its fame. History has taught us that, after the culmination of Tuscan and Roman art in Vasari's youth, a trend did set in which brought the 'Venetians' to the fore.

Vasari was thrilled by the works of Antonio Correggio, that great interpreter of joy and grace, that favoured master of the *chiaroscuro*, the dawn and twilight; lord, above all, of the beauty of flesh tints and richness of colouring. He could not conceive how such beauty could be created outside the artistic world of his own province. 'Correggio', he says, 'was blessed with a rare genius, a sublime painter who mastered the modern style of painting to such perfection that – gifted by nature and trained in art – he became in a few years a supreme artist. Certainly, no one handled colour better than he did. . . . ' Vasari describes admiringly Correggio's great church pictures, and also his female figures, whose superb nudity adorns many of the great galleries of Europe.

plate 51
p. 146

'Antonio,' says Vasari, 'burdened as he was with a family, always wanted to save money, but he had grown as poor as it is possible to be.' He tells how Correggio died of exhaustion in intense heat during a journey on foot; but neither the story of his poverty nor that of the manner of his death has stood the test of research.

Venice, when Vasari arrived there by way of Mestre, looked very much as it does today. The city's principal thoroughfare, the Grand Canal, had attained to its final form, fronted by the splendid palaces which may still be seen there. By San Marco, Vasari's architect-colleague Iacopo Sansovino was completing the 'Old Library', the 'Mint', and the Logetta at the foot of the Campanile. Even then the city was a lively centre, and the canals were crowded with ships, boats, and innumerable gondolas.

plate 18
p. 48

Vasari stayed with an old friend from Florence, a banker called Francesco Leoni, but was frequently and warmly received by Pietro Aretino, the productive and morally tarnished essayist, journalist, and

9 Vasari's parents, Antonio and Maddalena.
Portrait by Vasari.

10 Vasari's great-grandfather, Lazzaro, and
grandfather, Giorgio.

11 Nicolosa ('Cosina') di Francesco Bacci, Vasari's wife. Portrait by Vasari.

12 *Vasari and Cosina as SS Maddalena and Lazzaro.*   13 *Cosimo de' Medici, by Pontormo.*

14 *Bindo Altoviti, by Raphael.*

15 *Pope Clement VII, by Sebastiano del Piombo.*

16 *Cardinal Alessandro Farnese, by Titian (detail).*

17 *Cardinal Ippolito de' Medici, by Titian.*

Vincenzo Borghini.

18 *Paolo Giovio, woodcut by an unknown artist.*

19 *Vincenzo Borghini, engraving by A. Benaglia.*

20 *Pietro Aretino,*
engraving by Hollar after Titian.

21 *Benvenuto Cellini,*
engraving by Samuele Jesi after Vasari.

writer of comedies – 'phenomenally immoral', according to Gregoro-vius – who lived in princely style in one of the palaces alongside the canal, kept by his 'clients' or, if one will, his victims. He would certainly have been an excellent guide to the splendours of the city, if, indeed, he ventured to leave his home. For months at a time he would be obliged to remain indoors lest one of the many enemies he had incurred by his scribbling had him knifed by a hired bravo.

There were many things to see in the city, many artists to visit, and rich treasures of art to be studied. Social life flourished and there were all kinds of entertainments: parades, processions, carnivals, bear-baiting in the Piazza Sant' Angelo, and nocturnal festivals on the Grand Canal (the greatest of these, dedicated to *Il Redentore*, the Redeemer, was established a few years later), to say nothing of the great regattas, which had been kept up since 1315. During the principal events, the aquatic festivals, when the palaces by the canal were decorated with costly carpets and banners and tens of thousands of spectators encamped along the banks, there were countless ships, festooned and adorned with wondrous fabrics, and manned by magnificently attired youths. It is recorded by contemporary writers that 'hovering machines' were flown from some of these ships, bearing genii with divine attributes, while groups of tritons and nymphs sported below. The procession would be headed by the magnificently painted and gilded state galley of the repub-lic, *Il Bucintoro*. In theatres and private houses the Commedia dell' Arte and other plays were performed, and there were always concerts, given by talented amateur and professional singers, lutenists, and flautists.

It would have been uncharacteristic of Vasari if he had failed to do business here. Not much of the approximately ten months of his stay in Venice had elapsed before he had sold two pictures for 200 gold *scudi*. Besides assisting in the decoration and festive adornment of fashionable houses, he did, on the recommendation of the architect Sanmicheli, nine ceiling and wall pictures in the Palazzo Cornaro in oil – 'not inconsiderable', he says.

A large-scale project was obtained through Aretino. The latter, com-missioned by *La Compagnia della Calza*, who were preparing a celebration that was to cause a stir in the city's society, had written a comedy, *La Talanta*, and to Vasari was assigned the work of constructing the entire staging, on which he employed three of his men, chief among them his faithful assistant Cristofano Gherardi. In two months of labour they created a setting which came up to expectations. Vasari describes the work in a letter, written in 1542 to his friend and patron Ottaviano de' Medici, which tells us a good deal about middle-class tastes and aspirations. 'It was a very large hall,' Vasari says,

> a hundred and forty feet long and thirty-two feet wide. Along the walls we erected platforms for the ladies of the aristocracy, broken by niches containing busts. The walls and ceiling were decorated with pictures, representing a number of figures: Night, Aurora, Day, Evening, and the Hours. In addition there were Justice, Religion, Fame, Fortune, and Peace. Symbolical of Venice was a divinely beautiful Adria, quite naked, sitting on a rock in the sea, holding a branch of coral in her hand. Round about stood Neptune, Thetis . . . and other sea gods, bringing her precious stones, pearls, gold, and other treasures – all this for the most part completed by Cristofano.
>
> Above the pictures were cornices bearing architraves full of candles, and in front of these, large glass globes, filled with distilled water, caught the rays and so lit up the whole room. The stage chiefly showed views of Rome: a great many specimens of ancient and recent buildings – La Rotonda, the Colosseum, the Temple of Fortuna, Trajan's Column etc., together with beautiful palaces, houses, and churches containing a great many picturesque details of Doric, Ionian, Corinthian, Tuscan architecture – and a sun which, moving across the stage during the performance, produced an immense light by means of glass globes. . . .
>
> There was a huge throng of people, so that it was almost un-bearable in the hall, owing to the intense heat and the suffocating crowd. . . .

Both the staging and Aretino's comedy aroused great enthusiasm, privately as well as publicly.

Life in Venice clearly attracted Vasari, and the possibility occurred to him that he might stay there. 'Being now invited by the Venetian architect Michele Sanmicheli to settle in Venice,' he writes in the auto-biography, 'I might have decided to stay there for a year or two had not Cristofano dissuaded me, on the ground that the Venetians did not appreciate design, a failing for which the artists themselves were to blame. It was better to return to Rome, that true school of all noble arts, where talent itself is far better recognized than in Venice.'

Back in Rome, Vasari once more enjoyed the hospitality of Altoviti, and was soon fully employed. After being forced to leave the city with a fever induced by an intense heat wave, he returned and painted a *Pietà*, which made such a good impression that through it he came at last into contact with a man who belonged to the highest circles, Cardinal Alessandro Farnese. The Cardinal, a true scion of the arrogant, splen-dour-loving Farnese stock, was head of the papal administration; at the same time he did not neglect his wide-ranging private interests, the most important of which was the completion of the Palazzo Farnese under the direction of Sangallo and Michelangelo.

plate 16
p. 47

His Eminence gave Vasari a friendly reception and commissioned him to paint a picture, 'Justice', to adorn his office in the papal chancellery. (It is now in the Museo Nazionale, Pinacoteca, Naples.)

plate 23
p. 66

Vasari's own description of this work, which marks a turning-point in his career as a painter, conveys an impression of the contemporary addiction to stilted allegory, and the painting ideal of the fashionable person who commissioned it: 'The picture is a panel four *braccia* by eight (8 ft by 16 ft). Justice is grasping an ostrich, which bears the twelve tables of the Law. On her head she wears a crown of iron and gold, adorned with three feathers of different colours, symbols of the just judge; she is naked from the hips up. Fixed to her belt by means of golden chains are seven resisting captives symbolizing the seven vices: corruption, ignorance, cruelty, fear, treachery, falsehood and slander. Resting on their shoulders is the naked Truth, who is being led to Justice with a gift of two doves, symbolizing innocence; and Justice is crowning Truth with a wreath of oak-leaves, representing strength of

plate 24
p. 67

mind.' Delighted by the idea and by its execution, the Cardinal re-solved to have the great hall of the *Cancelleria* decorated, and gave Vasari the chance of his life by desiring him to depict a series of scenes from the life and works of the Cardinal's grandfather, Pope Paul III.

At the same time Vasari received many tokens of friendship and much good advice from Michelangelo, with whom he was once more in touch. 'Having seen some of my designs,' says Vasari, 'he induced me to turn once more to architecture and study it with great energy.' It was at this time, too, the spring of 1543, that the Cardinal urged Vasari to start on the *Lives*.

Vasari's first success as a monumental painter, the decorating of the great hall of the *Cancelleria*, included – besides many connecting compo-sitions and supplementary figures, decorative architecture, inscriptions, and so forth – four huge frescoes, which occupy the long wall and the two side walls, all with Pope Paul as the main figure. In the first picture he is seen in all his pomp, surrounded by his entire court, receiving am-bassadors of foreign nations and accepting tributes. In the next His Holiness is shown giving Virtue his reward, by distributing awards, knighthoods, prebends, episcopates, and cardinals' hats. Among the recipients are deserving men of the time, such as Cardinal Bembo, Paolo Giovio, Michelangelo, and 'other geniuses, drawn from life'. The third principal scene depicts Pope Paul, 'wholly engaged in build-ing enterprises, above all St Peter's and the Vatican. Kneeling before the Pope are Painting, Sculpture, and Architecture; these, symbolized in female figures, are unfolding a plan of the church, and receiving orders to carry out the work. Here also is the "Spirit of Enterprise", dis-playing in her opened breast her naked heart, and beside her are Soli-citude and Wealth . . .'; finally, in the last panel, is 'Universal Peace', established under the auspices of Christianity through Pope Paul – chiefly between Charles V and Francis, King of France, who are portrayed. Peace is burning arms, the Temple of Janus is being closed, and the ravages of war chained. In his description Vasari proudly adds, 'the whole work is full of mottoes and inscriptions, devised by Giovio, one of them telling that all these paintings were done in *a hundred days*'.

This gigantic work will strike most modern viewers as programme painting of a forced and theatrical type. The details are dry and have little spiritual ballast. A Swedish writer, Gregor Paulsson, says of this work: '. . . Paul III is glorified in the most obsequious manner. The fashionable court art of the fifteenth century has developed into cari/ cature/like servility.' One thing, however, cannot be gainsaid: it reveals its author's incredible inventiveness, and his ability to harmonize large decorated areas with monumental space.

At thirty/eight Vasari was still unmarried. Marriage ties were not popular with his artistic circle. Several times in his book he says that such/and/ such a colleague was 'burdened with a family'. But the time had now come for him to make a virtue of necessity. His growing self/confidence and discrimination made it difficult for him to find the right woman; but he had realized that if he wished to possess his own stately house, where he could lead a life of luxury and dignity, it would be well to have a worthy wife. He had asked some of his friends to look quietly around for a suitable match; he himself began to interest himself in a fellow/townswoman, Madonna Nicolosa di Francesco Bacci of Arezzo. During a visit to Cardinal Giovanni del Monte, a patron whom he was anxious not to offend, he came under strong pressure. 'The Cardinal', he relates, 'brought so many unanswerable arguments into play that I was persuaded to take a wife, a thing I had hitherto refused to do, and so, as the Cardinal wished, I took the daughter of Francesco Bacci, a noble citizen of Arezzo.' This is her first and last mention in the autobiography!

As Nicolosa found favour in the eyes of his friends – though the planned marriage aroused mixed feelings in them – Vasari entered into negotiations with his future father/in/law. Because of Giorgio's com/ bination of half/heartedness and exacting demands, they made slow progress and took about five years. His good friend Vincenzo Borghini was an extremely patient mediator, but had definite instructions to secure advantages—especially economic ones – for Giorgio in all respects.

plate 19
p. 48

In Vasari's correspondence we find letters which reflect his approach
to the enterprise. The cynical Giovio had sent the following warning:
'But I say, above all, do not take a wife in Rome, because there you are
sure to be cuckolded, and you might come to grief even though you
may not want to wear horns. And, since dowries are small in Arezzo,
Florence would suit you better. But do not aspire to the blood of the
counts Guidi, or Buondelmonti, or Uberti, which would give poor
marriage portions and bring tyranny into your house. I say, a match of
medium affluence . . . would please me more, for then you would
receive a nice dowry and be your own master, taking a wife without
conceit and arrogance. . . .'

And he returns to the subject in a later letter: '. . . This matter means
that you are putting up for sale the most precious thing possessed by
man, the beautiful freedom known only to him who has lost it and is
become a slave. And you, in taking a wife, must reflect on this, and on
the fact that you could have hung this yoke, the establishing of a household, on your brother's neck. But since Messer Simone tells me that
you are feeling the pinch, let me merely say: don't be in a hurry; don't
buy a pig in a poke; don't cast eyes on the dowry, because desire for that
breaks many a neck. But if the girl is good-looking and has caught you,
and the mother is jealous of her honour and virtue, then instead of
perpetual misfortune you will achieve domestic bliss. But, mind you,
count no more on getting away for an omelette at Monte Olivieri, for
wheaten bread at Cesano, or for indulgences in Rome! Oh, you might
say, I will stay in the shop and carry out the duties of marriage, in order
not to commit sin and contract the French disease. . . . But remember
that Andrea del Sarto had a vigorous wife, who would rather have had
two husbands than one! So, Messer Giorgio *mio*, have a mass said of
the Holy Ghost, cross yourself . . . and follow your cruel destiny.'

This took place, it is true, in 1549, long before the age of Romanti-
cism, yet even so, Vasari's own view of the matter is singularly cold and
egoistic. This is made abundantly clear by a letter written to Don Vincenzo, in which he enumerates his final demands, almost in the form of
an ultimatum: the 2,500 ducats which are to constitute the dowry 'do

not tempt him' (*sic*), but justice and his merit require it. Gifts and trousseau should correspond to the dowry and the status of the bride – and must not be deducted from the dowry. For the first two years his wife is to reside in her father's house, where Vasari will provide her with clothes, while her father will pay for her keep. She must not expect to live like a *principessa*, but occupy an unobtrusive position in the house. She must realize that he will always have to work and serve outside the home.

The diplomatic prior exhorts Vasari, in his reply, not to be too un-yielding . . . 'he cannot now withdraw, having regard for his fellow-citizens of Arezzo'; and his friend has nothing but praise for the bride, who is of a 'gentle, amiable, and compliant nature'.

Nicolosa, called by her family and friends 'Cosina', 'little thing', was, by all accounts, of a placid, cheerful disposition, as well as impec-cable chastity. She was obliged to remain in the Vasari house at Arezzo or in Florence while Giorgio travelled on his many financial and artistic interests – at the Curia, for that matter, one got on best without female relations – so that his friends had occasion to reproach him for neglect-ing his wife. She cared for him patiently when, overworked, he recuper-ated for a few days at home, and she sustained him in every way until, after twenty-four years of married life, she outlived him.

Of the few events in her life about which it is possible to glean in-formation in the letters, it is worth mentioning that Giorgio once struck a medal containing her portrait, and once, after twenty years of married life, allowed her to accompany him to Rome, where she was received by Pope Pius IV, who personally showed her the treasures of the Vatican.

Love seems to have had nothing to do with their marriage; and they had no children. The air of coldness is only momentarily warmed by a ray of sunshine – a sonnet to his wife, found among Vasari's letters, and reproduced overleaf.

In Vasari's house at Arezzo there is a well-preserved portrait of Cosina, very young and newly married, and flanked by two *gentildonne* of the town. In a later picture at Badia di Arezzo she is shown in stately

plate 11
p. 45

GIORGIO VASARI A SUA CONSORTE

Se 'l mio starti lontano a te dispiace,
    Consorte cara, a me dispiace e duole,
    Chè non si leva o colca in nel ciel sole
    Ch' io posi quest' affletta anima in pace.

Ardo tal' or qual' accesa fornace,
    M'agghiaccia ancor in bocca le parole,
    Divento come fredda neve al sole
    E nel fonte d'Epiro intinta face.

Pur vivo di speranza e di disio
    Di venir presto a te; or la mia vita
    Si parce d'ambasciate e di parole.

Se la speranza mia e tua, ch' in Dio
    Non fussi tal che mi porgessi aita,
    Dispererei di non lasciar prole.

plate 12
p. 46   classical costume and coiffure. The features are restrained and regular,
but the expression unsmiling.

From 1550 Vasari worked principally at Florence, and in the course of
a few years he transferred his household to that city and entered into
plate 13   permanent service with Duke Cosimo. This Medici, highly cultured
p. 46   as he was, was also full of enthusiasm for architecture and graphic art.
A firm and shrewd ruler, he could be ruthlessly ambitious, but he

GIORGIO VASARI TO HIS WIFE

If thou art grieved by my long journeying,
  My dearest wife, know how it saddens me.
  I pray the sun may never rise nor set
  Ere I find solace for my troubled heart.

Now leaps my soul like flames in furnace lit,
  Now freeze the words that form upon my lips;
  I am as snow before the sun's warm rays,
  A torch extinguished in Epirus' springs.

Now burns my heart with one desire and hope,
  That soon I may return to thee; my life
  Find consolation but in word of thee.

If all my trust and thine, reposed in God,
  Prove to be vain and I no succour find,
  Then vanish all our hopes of progeny.

avoided his predecessors' provocation of public opinion and warmly espoused general education and law and order. He was an ardent collector of antiquities, books, precious stones, medals, drawings, paintings and sculptures. Cosimo had an eye for Vasari's abilities, in particular his exceptional industry and outstanding organizational talent.

Vasari's regular salary was fixed at 300, later 450, ducats. Soon the Duke presented him with a house in Florence, in the fashionable Borgo Santa Croce, and another in the country; and he procured for him a true sinecure, in the office of *Gonfaloniere* at Arezzo (where he had already been made a member of the municipal corporation); this office he was not only permitted but actually ordered to administer through a deputy.

Fortune indeed seemed to be smiling on him. Commissions and good fees came pouring in. At Arezzo he bought a large house, half-built, in the Via di S. Vito (now the Via XX Settembre), and completed it himself with luxury and taste, decorating it outside and inside with his own hands. He painted on the ceiling of the main hall

plate 4
p. 18
plates 5, 6
p. 35

> thirteen large pictures, showing the gods of heaven and the four seasons; also, in the middle panel, Virtue treading Envy under foot, and, alongside, Fortune controlling them both, which at the time met with great approval. Going round the hall one comes, in turn, to Envy above Fortune, and, on the other side, Fortune above Envy – as one often sees this happen in real life. . . . I also depicted, among other things, all the provinces and cities where I had worked, with the idea that they had paid tribute to my house, through the income I had had there. . . . On the walls were Wisdom, Prudence, Industry and Honour, and on the ceiling design in every form. . . . At the entrance – for a joke – I painted a young woman holding a rake, indicating that she has raked up and brought with her as much as possible from her father's house [for once, a delightful piece of self-irony], and holding in her outstretched right hand – at her entry into her husband's house – a lighted torch to indicate that she is bringing fire which consumes and destroys everything (!)

The house was gradually filled with pictures (many by contemporaries), classical sculptures, and other objects of art. Furthermore, for two thousand ducats Vasari purchased a country estate in the Val di Chiana. As a token of the esteem in which he was held by his fellow-townsmen, they, the builders, and the canons of the church of S. Maria della Pieve decided to assign to him a chapel of his own, the one which is behind the high altar, and as a special grace the Pope granted him the necessary faculty in a bull *issued without charge*.

Inspired by this unprecedented honour, Vasari in 1563 applied himself to fitting out the chapel in the time-honoured Romanesque church, built in the twelfth and thirteenth centuries in the Piazza Grande (now called Piazza Vasari), Arezzo's central square. The altar was reconstructed from marble and porphyry, and crowned by a huge canopy. It was approached by five travertine steps surrounding the entire structure. On the altar was a tabernacle of the Blessed Sacrament, which could be reached from the front and the back, the altar having two altarpieces for that reason. On the side facing the nave he painted Christ calling the apostles Peter and Andrew, and on the one facing the apse he depicted four saints, over life-size, including his patron St George, all surrounded by a number of scenes from their lives, and a great many minor, sacred personages. On the base of the altar Vasari painted portraits of members of his family, whose bones he caused to be transferred to the chapel and buried below the altar.

Vasari availed himself of this favourable opportunity to repair other parts of the church, which he looked upon as his own. By clearance he provided more space for processions, by new windows better lighting; and he also put in new flooring. All this was made possible by the Duke's favour and grants, and by the friendship and admiration of the town's influential bishop. (In 1870 and the following years the church was restored to its original form, the mortal remains of Vasari and his family being removed to another part of it and the altar to the church of Badia in Arezzo.)

In these years – at the zenith of his life – Vasari had every reason for pride. Mighty works of building and decoration blossomed forth under his hands; his already admired new edition of the *Lives* was about to go to press; as the leading artist of the court he controlled, or vitally influenced, every artistic enterprise in Tuscany. His own chapel and the favour of the Church placed him in a flattering light as a devout and generous Christian; his wealth of estate, houses, objects of art, and gold ducats shed lustre on the good citizen Vasari. His pleasure and gratitude at his success are expressed in a letter to Duke Cosimo, quoted later in this book (p. 140).

These years were so full of work it seems well-nigh incredible that Vasari's strength and energy were equal to it. Moreover, in 1557 a great disaster overtook Florence. The Arno was swollen after violent rains and a great flood swept the city, carrying away houses, mills, and bridges; the beautiful Ponte di S. Trinità was totally destroyed, and only the Ponte Vecchio withstood the pressure entirely. The flooded river deposited quantities of gravel and ooze, which filled basements and ruined houses. There was also some loss of life. The Duke at once organized a large-scale relief action, distributed bread, wine and cloth-ing, and appointed a committee to make good the damage. Vasari, the obvious man to direct this undertaking, applied himself to it with his customary energy and with all his assistants from the Palazzo Vecchio, aided by Bartolomeo Ammannati, architect and sculptor – the man who rebuilt the Ponte di S. Trinità, which has since been described as the most beautiful bridge in Europe.

In Florence Duke Cosimo had entertained great plans with regard to the old residence, the Palazzo Vecchio. This stronghold, with its massive cube of rusticated walls and its audaciously slender tower, had over-looked the old city centre since its construction by Arnolfo di Lapo di Cambio at the beginning of the fourteenth century. After two hundred and fifty years the building was in sore need of restoration, especially inside. On the first floor were the apartments of the Duke. On the floor above were the private suite of the Duchess Eleonora, the audience chamber and the chapel. The third storey consisted of rooms for the children and the ducal staff. Facing the Piazza there was an open court-yard, which had been restored by Michelozzo in the fifteenth century. The rear part of the group of buildings, its three storeys enclosing a large courtyard, was a jumble of rooms and chambers, store-rooms, barracks, offices, reception rooms, guard-rooms, and – facing the Via de' Leoni – cages for the municipal lions. It was gloomy nearly everywhere, and important rooms were too low-ceilinged.

The palace superintendent, Giambattista Tasso, architect, carver, painter and carpenter, embarked upon a limited part of the plans, but proved unequal to the difficult task, was forced to neglect the work owing to illness, and then suddenly died. Vasari now took over. The entrance courtyard was splendidly redesigned and given its present columns. Inside, he provided space, design and orderliness by breaking through walls, doing away with rooms, straightening corridors and regulating staircases. An important innovation was a main staircase of one hundred and eighty steps through the entire height of the building.

In the midst of all this the Duke conceived a new plan, so bold that Vasari at first took it for a joke: in the great hall, later named the *Salone dei Cinquecento*, the roof and joists were to be raised thirteen *braccia* (about twenty-three feet) above their original level and a new and magnificent ceiling, decorated with wood-carving, gilding and paintings, was to be made. The Duke had had his doubts as to whether this was possible in the old building without serious risk of collapse, but Vasari undertook to prepare drawings and a large model. These were sent to Michelangelo in Rome, in order to get the opinion of the highest authority. When he gave the project his approval it was carried out, quickly and precisely, with Vasari's customary energy. The hall still makes an impressive effect on the beholder today.

plates 25–7 pp. 67, 68

All these works, which, as time passed, were steadily extended in scale, were supplemented with decorations of the Duchess's apartments, representing 'the great deeds of celebrated Greek, Roman, Hebrew and Tuscan women', and the colossal painting of the great hall, which was eighty *braccia* long and twenty *braccia* wide. Everything depended upon Vasari, who was soon feeling the weight of it all.

'It was a gigantic enterprise,' he says,

which if it did not exceed my will might exceed my powers. But whether it was my master's confidence or good fortune, which always went with him, which caused me to excel myself, or the anticipation and opportunity of a fine task which so greatly enhanced my powers, or – and I should have put this before all else – the grace of God which gave me strength, I took it upon me, and accomplished it!

All this I wished to relate merely in order to show with what exertion I worked – and work now – at my art, and on what reasonable grounds I could excuse myself if in any matter (in many, I think) I have failed.

The energetic Duke had long desired to provide new and convenient administrative quarters for his government and at the same time arrange for suitable rooms for the precious Medici art collections, and he had often discussed the matter with Vasari. Even before the completion of his work on the Palazzo Vecchio, Vasari was able, in 1560, to submit to the Duke drawings and estimates, together with a model in wood, for the combined structure, which was soon called the *Uffizi* (the offices).

plate 30
p. 78

On the site chosen for the building, rather larger as originally calculated than it was to turn out in the end, there had stood, ever since the beginning of the fourteenth century, a conglomeration of neglected, gloomy, dilapidated buildings, and Vasari's first estimate provided for the expropriation and removal of about three hundred houses – an enterprise from which even the lavish Duke recoiled. In the upshot forty-three houses, large and small, had to be demolished in order to provide space in the city centre and room for the Uffizi, and building began under the supervision of a committee of five, *I proveditori*, 'the providers'.

By the end of 1560 it was possible to cement the foundations, and among other objects deposited on the site was a specimen of a medal, struck for the occasion, and bearing the portrait of Cosimo and a sketch of the building, surrounded by the inscription *Publicae Commoditate*.

By 1564 the collecting of material and corrections for the second edition of the *Lives* was so far advanced that the elaborate printing, initially of the first two parts, could be started – to be finished, if possible, before the editing of the third and last part was concluded.

When the time approached for Vasari to complete his manuscript of the final part of the *Lives* he decided in 1566 to make a further long journey up and down Italy, estimated to take nearly four months, in order to 'see and see again' the country's works of art. Having obtained

leave of absence from the Duke and drawn up a will – a reasonable pre-
caution before such a big and perhaps risky venture – and after depositing
this with Borghini, he set out, first for Arezzo, where his wife was left
at the Casa Vasari, and thence, *via* Cortona, Perugia, and Assisi, for
Rome. After a week there he proceeded northward by way of Rimini,
Ravenna, Bologna, Parma, Modena and Milan to Mantua, where he
enjoyed the lavish hospitality of his friend Giulio Romano. He then
continued his journey to Verona and Venice, where he stayed for five
days.

It was indeed an impressive feat, travelling on horseback, with pack,
an average of about thirty miles a day; and on the way, as he says,
'seeing everything'.

After his return Vasari was summoned to Pisa, where the Knights
of the Order of San Stefano had decided to build a house for the order,
as well as a church with campanile – which will be further discussed in
the next chapter of this book. It was a task which claimed most of his
working energy until 1569. In that year he felt obliged to obey a summons from Rome, where the Pope, now Pius V, wished him to paint
three chapels in the Vatican, dedicated respectively to SS. Peter Martyr,
Stephen and Michael.

When this important work had been done, and he had inspected
works in Florence and Bosco and concluded his personal work in Pisa,
he found time to design a monumental tomb for Michelangelo. This,
which is in the church of Santa Croce in Florence, to the right of the
entrance, is a large structure of partly polychrome marble decorated with
the master's emblem – three intertwined wreaths, symbolizing the three
arts – and a portrait bust by Batista Lorenzi. Today the monument does
not seem inspired, and leaves the viewer rather cold.

Although again possessed by a furious zest for work, on church
building, decorating rooms, designing furnishings, private panels and
portraits, Vasari managed at this time to put the finishing touches to the
completed, illustrated edition of the biographies, which then went to
press. The title of the book was changed, the painters being now placed
first. Among the additional artists included are a number of his con-

plate 2
p. 17

temporaries, colleagues then still alive, and the work concludes with his autobiography.

For some years the idea of establishing an Academy of the Fine Arts had been mooted in Florentine artistic circles. There had existed in the city since 1346 a guild company, *La Compagnia et Fraternità di San Luca*, with the principal objects of religious observance and mutual relief. With Vasari as the prime mover, a group of artists, among them Ammannati and Bronzino, founded in 1563 *L'Accademia del Disegno*, the oldest academy to be regularly constituted and legally recognized. Three hundred years later it was incorporated in the *Istituto di Belle Arti* of the Kingdom of Italy. The work of the Academy was directed by six Consuls, elected for half-yearly terms, and the *ex officio* President was Duke Cosimo. A few years later it fell to Vasari, as Consul, to propose for membership an impressive array of artists from Venice: Titian, Paolo Veronese, Tintoretto and Iacopo Sansovino.

In the initial period this academy, which numbered about seventy members, met in rooms belonging to the church of San Lorenzo, the hospital and the chapel; later Giovan-Angelo Montorsoli, sculptor and Servite friar, assigned a chapel, instituted by him at the church of Santa Annunziata, for the use of the fraternity.

The indefatigable Vasari again obeyed a summons to Rome, where he was commissioned by the new Pope, Gregory XIII, to decorate the *Sala Regia* in the Vatican, and here, close to the Sistine Chapel, largely with the help of assistants, he did seven 'histories', among them the excommunication of Emperor Frederick II by Pope Gregory IX, the same Pope's return to Rome after the exile at Avignon, the celebrated Battle of Lepanto in the reign of Pius V in 1571, and, as one of the great deeds of the Church, the massacre of St Bartholomew. The battle-piece, he wrote to Borghini, was 'the most beautiful of all my works . . . which will make me famous'. After this feat he was obliged to return to Tuscany, but stayed at Arezzo on the way, to be cared for at home by Cosina following his incredible exertions. He remained there for ten days, and after a couple of weeks in the country was back in Florence,

*22 Lorenzo de' Medici
('the Magnificent')
—one of the few good
portraits Vasari painted.*

23 Vasari's allegorical 'Justice', painted for Cardinal Farnese.

24 *Scenes from the life of Pope Paul III: frescoes by Vasari in the Cancelleria.*

25 *Vasari's paintings in the Palazzo Vecchio, Florence—'a gigantic enterprise'.*

26 Pope Leo X in the College of Cardinals: painting by Vasari in the Palazzo Vecchio.

27 Pope Clement VII and the Emperor Charles V: painting by Vasari in the Palazzo Vecchio.

there – his confidence in his powers undiminished – to set to work on another great task, the painting in fresco of the interior of the cathedral dome.

Having for a year laid every other work aside, he managed to complete a series of prophets in the lantern, but after the death of his friend and principal, Duke Cosimo, in April 1574, he seems to have lost his vitality and finally to have been forced to give up. There is no available information about any well-defined illness, but he suffered from 'chronic catarrh', which made him breathless and fatigued. Much against his will he had to break off his work, and after about ten days in bed at home in the Borgo Santa Croce he died on the 27th of June, after a lifelong, hard-working achievement in his art, missed by friends and not least by his exacting clients. Vasari was temporarily buried in Florence, but after the lapse of several years his body was taken, with great ceremony, to Arezzo and interred with those of his forebears below the altar in his own chapel in the Pieve di Arezzo.

None of his associates possessed sufficient artistic authority to be entrusted with the completion of the work in the cathedral, a task which fell to a 'foreigner', the Roman painter Federico Zuccari.

Vasari left no children; the name died out with a great-grandchild of his brother Pietro, Francesco Maria Vasari, Cavaliere di Santo Stefano, in 1687.

In his will Vasari had directed that after the male line of his family became extinct all property in land and buildings should pass to the charitable guild of *La Fraternità dei Laici* at Arezzo (an ancient lay fraternity associated with the clergy), all personal property to be spent on legacies for unmarried daughters of artisans in Florence, in portions of 50 *scudi*. All papers were to go to *La Fraternità*, but most of these – as related elsewhere in this book – were lost for two hundred years. His widow was to have a share of the landed properties, a home in the house at Arezzo, and 500 florins. But the sum of 800 florins, the portion of her dowry which remained unpaid, was to be deducted from her inheritance!

Chapter III

Fame and Fortune

I T I S difficult to understand now why Vasari was so admired and sought after as a painter. His patrons and clients were the best: the Medici showered favours on him, as did the rich nobility; churches and monasteries commissioned him again and again; he worked for the highest ecclesiastical dignitaries, including five Popes and as many cardinals. He tells us in his book that he had to decline an engagement by the King of France – for one reason or another he never went abroad. Unquestionably, his work became fashionable.

He was so familiar with the mythological, biblical, and historical background to the current subjects of painting, as well as contemporary allegory and symbolism, that he was personally able to conceive and suggest ideas for pictures, including the character and costume of the figures and the architectural and landscape setting. The over three hundred studies made in his youth came in useful to him at all times. His clients, unaccustomed perhaps to such preparation in other artists, were invariably delighted to clinch the deal at once. Moreover, there was the extraordinary speed with which he completed even the biggest of commissions, his sound technique of colouring, plastering, fresco painting and stucco modelling, his masterly co-ordination of every aspect of the work, the supervision of his assistants, and the precision and promptness with which he was able to secure deliveries.

Vasari was an indefatigable and extraordinarily industrious worker, incessantly on the move from assignment to assignment, from city to city. In his autobiography he records a score of visits to Rome, a like number of periods spent in Florence and Arezzo, and working journeys and study visits to Pisa, Venice, Padua, Naples, Verona, and over twenty other localities and communities. He seems to have endured the hardships and dangers of this life of travel unharmed. War and unrest were never far away and (except in Tuscany) robbers lay always in wait for travellers who were inadequately provided with costly protection. This, however, Vasari invariably had by virtue of his distinguished connections, who got him permission to accompany the mail: unlike his contemporary, Benvenuto Cellini, who says that he was frequently obliged to set out by night in order to elude footpads and hired assassins, and that he continually had to ward off attacks by dagger and sword.

Of Vasari's vast output as a painter only a scant proportion is admired today. His pictures differ strikingly in quality. Most of them are done with undoubted craftsmanship, often with great skill in drawing; many have great formal qualities of composition. In this respect they reveal the influence of his great master, Michelangelo: but the spark of genius, alas, is not there.

In his biggest works, such as the colossal decorations of the Palazzo Vecchio, with the vast halls which bear the names of 'heroes of the Medici family', princes, Popes, dukes, he executed forty elaborate compositions, and in them we find an incredible array of figures, nude, in every period costume, or in allegorical dress. Vasari says of these: 'I venture to assert that I had occasion to paint everything that the human mind and imagination can envisage: a multitude of bodies, faces, costumes, dresses, helmets, cuirasses, headdresses, horses, armour, breastplates, artillery of every kind; combats, battles, ships, storms, rain, snow, and so forth.'

The invention, though grandiose, is often cramped, the posing of the figures forced, the gestures vapid; the expressions on the faces often seem vacant. His women's faces are coquettish, devoid of real life or feeling, let alone passion: in short, they are dull. Many of the large church pictures one would now, at the most, call fair.

In some of the large pictures the effect is weakened by the fact that the main figures, whether a prince or a Pope, are somewhat lost in the welter of minor figures; or they occupy a humble position in the back

ground, the foreground being filled by portraits of cardinals, other mag‚
nates, or allegorical figures. A 'Birth of Christ', now in the Galleria
Borghese, is a Christmas crib of a tableau; an 'Amor and Psyche',
jauntily ballet‚like. This picture ended up in Berlin, where it may have
been lost but will not be missed.

The portraits, especially of men, are better. Vasari painted many of
these – on wood, canvas, walls, in tempera, in oils, and especially in
fresco: the Medici family, Popes and foreign princes, rich men and fellow‚
artists. Some of them reveal a good grasp of features and character,
plate 22 among the best being the picture of Lorenzo the Magnificent and the
p. 65 self‚portrait in the Uffizi. The portraits of Michelangelo, Andrea del
Sarto and Ghiberti also display skill in characterization. But it is obvious
that both he and his patrons overrated his work. If his productions
were to a large extent mediocre, the reason – apart from the abuse of his
talent – may be the fact that he was always in too great a hurry. It is
said that when he showed Michelangelo his vast fresco in the Can‚
celleria in Rome, proudly declaring that he had done it all in a hundred
days (the great hall has since been called *Sala dei Cento Giorni*), the
great man drily observed: 'Yes, so I see!' Speed entailed the employment
of a large number of assistants and apprentices, and under such condi‚
tions inspiration would obviously be lacking. Some of his friends were
aware of this fault. Annibale Caro, for example, wrote to him: '. . .
above all, be not in a hurry; for "the cat in a hurry catches the smallest
mice." ' That he himself in his maturity had his doubts is indicated by
an observation in the autobiography concerning the work in the Can‚
celleria: ' . . . though I laboured much, I confess that I was wrong in
giving it into the hands of assistants in order to finish everything quickly;
it would have been better had I worked on it for a hundred months –
and done it all myself.'

Although he regarded himself chiefly as a painter, Vasari was to
achieve his greatest work as an architect. Under the stimulus and
patronage of Michelangelo, he created significant works in this art.
For example, he planned and designed for Cardinal del Monte, later
Pope Julius III, every detail of the beautifully situated and in every

respect admirable *Vigna* – afterwards generally known as the Villa
Giulia, and now an Etruscan museum – which stands in a corner of the
Borghese Gardens, outside the Porta del Popolo in Rome. This build
ing project, usually associated with Vignola, owed its origin to Vasari.
He records that he studied the cardinal's innumerable desires and ideas
with him from the outset, formulating them and putting them on
paper. For assistants he had his approximately contemporary col
leagues, Bartolomeo Ammannati and Iacopo Barozzi, the latter com
monly known as Vignola after the town where he was born. Both of
these did outstanding independent work, but, to all appearances, for
a period under the supervision of Vasari. Items found in Vasari's
accounts give Vignola's monthly salary as thirteen gold *scudi*.

plate 31
p. 95

Vasari hoped to obtain regular work from the Pope, but this did not
materialize. 'With him,' Vasari says, 'one had to remain in hopes, and
one strove in vain in his service. . . .' Consequently he broke off,
allowed his assistants to complete the Villa Giulia, and went to Florence.

In the year 1561 and thereafter Duke Cosimo carried out a plan in
tended both to shed lustre on the Medici rule and to create an effective
support for the State: the institution of the Order of Santo Stefano.
With the Pope's blessing, the statutes were signed on the martyred St
Stephen's day (on which day the Duke also commemorated two of
his victories). Members were to be drawn from the nobility, who were
to be tempted with insignia, habits – a white cloak with a large red
cross, the mark of the old Order of St John of Jerusalem – privileges,
and stately buildings as the domicile of the order. The members were
expected to uphold the ideals of chivalry, to support the dynasty and the
Roman Catholic Church with all their means, and to guard against,
and when necessary fight against, foreign enemies, especially Barbary and
other pirates who threatened from the sea. For the pacification of poten
tial trouble-makers at home among the nobility, however, as well as
for mutual benefit, the order was to be subject to the Duke as grand
master for life.

The chosen domicile was the port of Pisa, and the Duke, who had
provided lavish endowments, turned to that obvious master of great

enterprises, his very devoted supporter Vasari, who was granted a pro-
visional budget of 15,000 ducats. The quietly situated Piazza delle
Sette Vie, close to the cathedral, the Leaning Tower and the *Camposanto*, was chosen for the site and was renamed Piazza dei Cavalieri di
Santo Stefano. Here, in the following years, Vasari completed three
considerable buildings. The first was a convent house for the knights,
called the Palazzo della Carovana (now a school); this was beautifully
planned, with a noble flight of steps leading to the front, and was embellished with busts of the six princely founders of the order. To the
left, he built a residence for the dignitaries of the order, containing rooms

plates 32, 33
p. 95

for an infirmary and a dispensary; a gravely harmonious building, severe
in style, which was formerly called Il Palazzotto and has been commonly
known later as Il Palazzo dell' Orologio. Finally, he built a chapel for
the order, together with a *Canonica*. The chapel, which stands on the
right, has a grandiose but not very inspired exterior, while the interior
presents a majestic appearance in a Venetian-Vasari style, having great
width and large areas of white walls. The walls are decorated with
monochrome frescoes by Vasari and are hung with war trophies, the
many time-honoured banners captured in the Turkish wars in particular
giving the room a peculiarly attractive atmosphere. The whole exem-
plifies Vasari's unflagging energy and direction, especially when we
bear in mind that he had numerous other irons in the fire at the same
time.

As part of the struggle to uphold the power and prestige of the
Church, the Duke conceived it his duty to preserve the fame and the
glory of the principal churches. He felt dissatisfied with the interiors of
Santa Maria Novella and Santa Croce, and again his factotum Vasari
had to bear the brunt. 'In Santa Maria, he [the Duke] got me to remove
the screen, which spoilt the whole beauty of the church, and provide
a rich new choir behind the high altar.' In Vasari's opinion, the
alterations made Santa Maria Novella a wonderful new church.

Also at the Duke's orders, Vasari built a number of chapels, which
were richly decorated in a new style. It is difficult to assess the value of
such changes now, and they have inspired mixed feelings. At any rate,

it has been deeply deplored that Vasari, at the duke's behest, should have undertaken similar alterations to the great church of Santa Croce in Florence, removing the screen and placing the choir behind the high altar, which in turn was brought slightly forward. As in Santa Maria, a series of chapels was built along the wall, which had to be white washed, with the result that precious frescoes were destroyed. Vasari also demolished the old monks' choir which occupied the central part of the basilica. The verdict of modern times is that this was sheer vandalism.

Let us examine Vasari's largest individual piece of architecture, familiar to all who have visited Florence: the Uffizi. In his own account of it, Vasari says that 'because of the situation, the building entailed an extremely difficult foundation – in the river itself, so to speak.'

The Uffizi comprises two three storey oblong wings enclosing an almost rectangular courtyard, open to the Piazza della Signoria and connected on the side facing the River Arno. The two wings, if a trifle heavy, make an extremely harmonious effect by reason of their broken façades. In these the architect, inspired by Sanmicheli, employs a rhythmical division, the windows of the upper storeys being grouped in threes. Correspondingly, the ground floor, which forms one long loggia, is divided by groups of two lightish columns and one massive pillar. On the Arno side the wings are linked by a loggia, which is supported by columns and crowned by a harmonious Palladian arch. The architectural features mentioned reappear in two works at Arezzo, the Badia church and the Palazzo alle Colonne. In the Badia, which was founded in the fourteenth century, but which Vasari entirely rebuilt internally about 1550, he achieved in this way an imposing effect in the aisles and chapels. The Palazzo alle Colonne, commenced in the last year of his life for La Fraternità dei Laici, and containing offices, an assembly hall, and for many years a theatre, graces with its quiet style and its restrained monumentality the venerable Piazza Grande – the Piazza Vasari, as it is often called today.

It also fell to Vasari's lot to construct the large, enclosed corridor, Il Corridoio Vasariano, which connects the Uffizi by way of the Ponte

plate 30
p. 78

plate 3
p. 18

Vecchio with the new ducal residence, the Palazzo Pitti. He completed this in a little more than five months – a work which, in his own opinion, might have been expected to take five years. The entire length, from the Uffizi to the Pitti, is about half a mile.

Vasari was in many respects favoured by fortune, or rather by fortunate circumstances – though this does not apply absolutely to his development as an artist. His original talent and his youthful bent lay in the direction of Michelangelo's classicism, but his path to independent maturity was anything but a straight one. His admired Raphael had died before he started; his studies under Luca Signorelli, Andrea del Sarto and Michelangelo were too brief for him to become fixed in the classical style.

For a long time he had to content himself with Michelangelo's unfortunate imitator, the sculptor Baccio Bandinelli, for his mentor. Though a good draughtsman and an energetic teacher, the latter was a somewhat unattractive character. Vasari describes him, by all accounts correctly, as an insufferable, self-assertive crank: from which it follows that, draughtsmanship apart, he cannot have had much influence on the development of his pupil's artistic development. Outward success was an impediment to such development in the receptive years of Vasari's youth. There is also the fact, which will be discussed below, that for various reasons he was drawn into the atmosphere of reaction against the High Renaissance which formed after the 1520s and 1530s.

During the great study tour of 1541–42 Giorgione, Titian, and the other great Venetians inspired Vasari with warm admiration. Recognizing the aura and the colouring which distinguished this school, he could, if his fate had been otherwise, have stayed on in Venice and acquired the Venetian manner, which proved to be far more durable than the Roman-Florentine. But his career in Tuscany drew him back home, and he could not resist a conviction of 'defective draughtsmanship' in the Venetians. Consequently, he did not avail himself of the opportunity and returned home without being deeply influenced by the Veneto.

28 'La Maestà', Simone's great fresco in the Town Hall of Siena.

29 Cimabue: Madonna and Child, surrounded by angels and St Francis.

30 The Uffizi ('the offices'), designed by Vasari for Duke Cosimo to house the Medici art collections and the offices of the Duke's government.

He returned not only to his native region but also to the artistic milieu where he belonged: that of Mannerism. The art-historical aspects of this movement have invested the period with an importance far transcending the time and the place. It will help towards an understanding of Vasari and his work if we pause to consider it.

For centuries in the history of art the term Mannerism has been applied, with the effect of a slogan, to an artistic trend whose exponents were the direct and indirect successors of Raphael and Michelangelo. The Italian *Maniera*, meaning 'manner', denotes an artist's manner of painting, or personal style. From it is derived the pejorative term *manierato*: that is, 'mannered' or 'affected'. Mannerism in painting is the term applied to the decadence noted in the generations of painters that succeeded the great ones, chiefly centred in the first place on Florence and Rome but afterwards spreading to the whole of Italy and through France and Germany to most of Europe, and fixed chronologically between 1520 and the close of the century.

Almost down to the present day, art critics were contemptuous of this school; its representatives were regarded as nothing but crude imitators of Raphael and Michelangelo, their manner of painting an unattractive and degenerate trend. The classical ideals were so firmly established that any attempt to seek new paths seemed inevitably to be sidetracking. Yet in Vasari's day Italian painting throve exceedingly; there was full employment for talents great and small, and fees flowed freely.

Earlier literature on art, greatly indebted to Vasari's *Lives*, regarded the painting of the High Renaissance as the culmination of all time. Generally speaking, it saw only the Mannerist break with the traditional theory of proportion and its abandonment of the requirement of harmony in figures, space, and general composition, of 'beauty of style' in general. Mannerist figures were found to be distorted, grossly contorted and foreshortened, cramped in space, erratic and unbalanced, and overloaded with contrived attributes and allegories.

The art literature of the Mannerist period and the immediately succeeding one sees little positive importance in these artists. A few authors besides Vasari – among them Lomazzo and Federico Zuccari –

suggest that something new, something different had arisen in painting. It is only in the last generation that critics have applied new criteria to this whole question, believing that for far too long this interesting period has received unfair treatment. At the turn of the century a number of authors began to realize that Mannerism was composed of more than mere imitation of the great predecessors.

The first important contribution was made by the German scholar Hermann Voss, who in 1920 published a book which contained the results of extensive studies of Mannerist art, or Late Renaissance art, as he calls it. He gives an affirmative answer to the question whether the period calls for a reappraisal, following the general disregard in which it has been held. Voss, pointing to the over-ripeness to which the High Renaissance attained in the works of Giulio Romano, Perino del Vaga and others, sees the development of a new phase in Mannerism. In Florence this style was evident already in Pontormo, Rosso Fiorentino and Vasari, and was developed by pupils of Bronzino and Vasari until, at the close of the sixteenth century, individualists like Barocci, Santi di Tito and the Carracci created a reformation in the art of painting.

While repeatedly pointing out the Mannerists' lack of originality, the feebleness of their figure drawing, and their overloaded compositions, Voss concludes that their achievement, and particularly that of Salviati and Vasari, was of lasting importance, because 'instead of following a set pattern, they ventured to study different trends and fuse the Florentine with the Roman, and indeed with that of all northern Italy.' Of Vasari he says: 'Wherever his eventful life led him he heralded the grandly decorative ideal of the Roman school. . . . The history of art can point to examples of personalities who have won their place less by the tangible results of their endeavour than by the significance and intensity of that endeavour, whether as precursors of something greater to come, or as tireless champions and propagators of new ideas already translated into decisive action. One such convinced and courageous protagonist was Vasari.'

In Italy Mannerism for long had a 'poor press'. Adolfo Venturi in his great handbook treats the period with chill neutrality; G. E. Mottini, in his widely read and much quoted work, *Storia dell' Arte Italiana* (1949), says of Michelangelo's successors, Daniele da Volterra, Vasari, Marcello Venusti and others: 'They imitated him without understanding him, and could do no more than imitate the outward appearance of the figures, the muscular violence, and the foreshortenings. . . .' Bernard Berenson, eminent for two generations as a connoisseur of Italian Renaissance art, observes of Raphael's followers: 'No wonder that we have given over Giulio Romano, Perino del Vaga, Giovan Francesco Penni, Polidoro da Caravaggio, and their ignoble fellows to oblivion. It is all they deserve.' (*The Italian Painters of the Renaissance*, London, 1952.)

Voss provoked a lively debate among art historians, with the object of discussing and elucidating the intellectual basis of this once despised period, illuminating its thoughts and their pictorial representation.

In 1927 a Swedish scholar, Henrik Cornell, called for a new approach to Mannerism. In his *The Late Renaissance of Italy: Sculpture and Paintings* (Stockholm, 1927) he writes: 'This art indeed approaches the focal point of art-historical interest, thanks to the contribution which it makes towards elucidating important problems of art history. . . . It is one of the great epochs, characterized by what may be called a turning to the idea, an orientation of art away from the individually received world of the senses to a world created or recreated by man himself. . . . . But even more important is the disregarding of atmosphere and space that is bound up with the whole abstract approach.' Of Pontormo's frescoes in the Certosa, he says: 'its [Mannerism's] inner aspiration is realized here more manifestly and more radically than perhaps at any time later.'

At about the same time as Cornell's work came that of Max Dvořák (*Geschichte der italienischen Kunst*, Munich, 1927–28), which endeavours in its own way to define the characteristic features of Mannerism. Viewing it as an historical phenomenon, he argues that it should be seen, not merely as an intermediate phase between Renaissance and Baroque, but as a more universal conception. Instead of the objectivism of the Renaissance, Mannerism expressed a view which we may term 'individualistic subjectivism'. 'If', he says, 'we apply another criterion than that of naturalism, judging art by the life of the imagination which it embodies, then the structure of art history hitherto employed is completely changed, and periods formerly regarded as decadent are transformed into peaks of development, or at least periods of the most fruitful ideas. . . . We have not previously been aware that here was a period of formative importance for the whole of our modern time. . . . This importance is due primarily to the subordination of material views to psychologically subjective ones, rooted in the inner life, views which are more permanent and more universal than the former ones.'

Dvořák awards Mannerism a place among the ideas and currents of the sixteenth century which are of European importance, along with the Counter-Reformation and the contemporary reorientation of the social, ethical, philosophical and literary life.

In 1937 the Swedish art historian Gregor Paulsson (*The Italian Renaissance, II: Sixteenth Century*. Stockholm, 1937) adduced two factors which briefly characterize Mannerism: a negative one which consists in a dissolution of the harmony of the High Renaissance, so that the details, the manner, receive attention at the cost of the whole; and a positive one, consisting in a highly subjectivist attitude to nature. These factors he sees as the decisive criterion of Mannerism, which thus manifests itself as a reaction against the Renaissance.

In the recent literature an account of the history and character of Mannerism is given by Giuliano Briganti (*Il Manierismo e Pellegrino Tibaldi*. Rome, 1945). He recalls that it was always regarded as an evil (*un male*) that had befallen Italian art, since it was considered 'cold, anaemic, and uninspired'. 'But', he says, 'what it amounts to is a matter of weeding out false definitions and demonstrating that the basis of the negative view of Mannerism, its inclusion as part of a closed Renaissance-Baroque system, for example, is false.'

Briganti finds the Mannerist artists mutually related in their unrest, their mental stress, their sensitivity, and their tendency to sensualism and mysticism. 'They are highly intellectual in expression, and their style is formalistically elegant.'

It is evident that in their painting the Mannerists wished to deal with 'philosophical matters' and abstract subjects, which they illustrated by means of involved and profound allegories, a desire which led inevitably to the 'scholarly artist' type, such as Vasari. They fostered a form of composition which demonstrates the intellectual and the virtuoso. In their innumerable 'stories' or *storiette* their treatment of gestures and attitudes bordered on the fantastic; yet it must be admitted that the style indicates a new taste, a new sensibility, a new way of apprehending and expressing things.

It is an interesting fact, noted by several of the authors mentioned, that the basic origins of Mannerism can be traced to the later works of Michelangelo himself, including the best known of these, the 'Last Judgment' in the Sistine Chapel. Here, 'instead of the objective substance outside man,' as Dvořák puts it, we find 'a tendency towards pictorial embodiment of the subjective experiences of art – values drawn by him from his inner life.'

The debate on the value of Mannerism is by no means over – on the contrary, one may say. It flares up persistently in European art history with fresh pros and cons. One manifestation of this interest has been the holding of large representative exhibitions of Mannerist works, as, for example, in Amsterdam in 1955, from where a voice was heard proclaiming the 'triumph of Mannerism'. The following year, on the occasion of the 400th anniversary of the death of Pontormo, an exhibition of works by Pontormo and early Florentine Mannerists was held in the Palazzo Strozzi in Florence, where it attracted considerable interest.

Many reasons for the controversy are apparent. As painters, the Mannerists differ greatly in quality, and the actual Mannerist substance of their works is of very different merit. In some the composition becomes a tableau, dignity a pose, passion sentimentality, or drama theatricality – and this can occur even in the best of them. Such weaknesses must bear part of the blame for the disrepute which Mannerism still has difficulty in transcending in wider circles. But in considering the positive aspects of Mannerism it must also be borne in mind that its basic tendencies are not confined entirely to the latter half of the sixteenth century. Always in good painting there have been subjectivity and abstraction; we sense it in the Trecentists and the Quattrocentists, not least in Leonardo and the great Venetians from Giorgione and Titian to Tintoretto, El Greco, Sebastiano del Piombo and Parmigianino. But it is definitely to the credit of Mannerism that it explored and accentuated these concepts, in such a way and at such a time as to cause repercussions through Impressionism and Expressionism down to our own time, when pure abstraction – in the extreme – is breaking the final links with objectivism.

Vasari's position in the Mannerist school of painting presents several aspects. That he belonged to it was almost a matter of course. He became acquainted with the style of Andrea del Sarto in his early youth; the latter's pupils, Pontormo and Rosso Fiorentino, both lent him a helping hand in his first years of painting, and the outstanding younger Mannerists, Salviati, Bronzino, and Giulio Romano, were all his valued colleagues and close friends. Yet Vasari never became a profound, spiritual painter like Pontormo (whose famous Certosa works repelled him), but rather a 'scholarly painter'. He undoubtedly believed that he was following Raphael and Michelangelo in his works, and he found it difficult to depart from the 'style beautiful' and disregard space and atmosphere – nor indeed was he the one to create a reaction against Michelangelo. I have already mentioned how, perhaps to a greater extent than any other painter, he went in for the decorative mass effect, stopping at nothing in the presentation of human figures in crowds, in distortions and foreshortenings, in the midst of combat, triumph and passion, subject to the whims of every element, and richly provided with allegorical adornments. His entire output of paintings rests on his remarkable knowledge of history, mythology, religion and legend, which emphasizes the literary and intellectual aspect of his stories.

What Vasari personally failed to contribute to the sphere of Mannerism was largely provided by his pupils, who were to figure in a diluted Mannerism. The best known of them were Bernardo Buontalenti, Giovanni Stradano, Iacopo Zucchi, and Alessandro del Barbiere.

There is no systematic account in the writings of Vasari of the style of painting which we now call Mannerist; he describes his colleagues of the period individually, according to their professional skill. But here and there in his literary works we come across observations which touch on the Mannerist idea and programme.

The other 'writer-painter', Federico Zuccari, has been praised for drawing attention to 'intrinsic' design and the need for consonance between nature and art; but Vasari had done this long before in the *Lives* when writing of *disegno* as a universal principle. He sees subjectivist features in Masaccio, Andrea del Sarto and Leonardo, but does not interpret them as significant. On the subject-matter of paintings he expresses himself – in full accordance with his pictures – altogether Manneristically. He says in the *Ragionamenti* that 'it is permissible for the brush to treat philosophical subjects as narrative, since poetry and painting, as sisters, employ the same expressions'. Writing to his learned friend Benedetto Varchi, he says: 'It (the painting) perfectly represents the plains, rivers, storms, rain, thunder, lightning, night, clear sky, moonlight and starshine, the sun and its rays. . . . It renders folly and wisdom in the faces . . . the dead with bleeding wounds, variations of flesh tints and garb . . . the fineness of the hair and beard . . . all according to the will of the practised hand and the memory of the good artist.' His notebook, *Lo zibaldone di Giorgio Vasari*, preserved in the Vasari archives at Arezzo, contains lists of attributes and allegorical elaborations of all manner of conceptions: love, virtue, vice, vanity, doubt, grief, calumny, mendacity, truth, ignorance, wisdom, happiness, envy, war, peace, and so forth.

Even when discussing, in the *Lives*, his 'third period', the classical climax, he speaks of 'the seen and unseen', and of the grace which eclipses the merely regular – all ennobled through *disegno*.

In his ideas Vasari thus to some extent anticipates the future conception of Mannerism.

Looking back on Vasari's career as a painter, we have to admit that he failed to achieve the artistic supremacy to which he aspired. His knowledge, his professionalism, his inventiveness, and his technical grasp of large-scale works were legendary. In this respect his good fairies, Fame and Fortune, placed him among the great; but his fates, Invidia and Nemesis, prevented him from expressing the inexpressible, in his hundreds of pictures, with such true inspiration as could be created in a few works by Giotto, Masaccio, or Giorgione.

As an architect, however, Vasari achieved a much surer position. The trend of this art was along steadier and more certain paths. In Florence a rich heritage had been left by the outstanding artists of the fifteenth century. The works of Filippo Brunelleschi had become famous, his bold cathedral dome being a marvel of the age and his loggia for the Foundling Hospital and chapel in Santa Croce, built for the Pazzi, seeming to contemporaries – as they have seemed to posterity – gems of subtlety. The latter half of the century is deeply imprinted with the master spirit of Leon Battista Alberti. He had embodied his intense feeling for the ancient world in characteristic works in many cities, particularly in an epoch-making work in Florence, the Palazzo Rucellai. The principal work of Michelozzi, the Palazzo Medici (later called the Palazzo Riccardi), also contributes to the city's appearance today. At the close of the Quattrocento, two architects appeared who were to influence the art of building for a hundred years: the brothers Giuliano and Antonio Giamberti, both of them celebrated under the name of Da Sangallo.

When Vasari appeared on the scene, young and receptive, his mind was inevitably influenced by such splendid achievements; and after he had witnessed the work of Michelangelo in the Biblioteca Laurenziana and the Medici sacristy of San Lorenzo, it followed as a matter of course that the influence of great architecture impressed itself upon him permanently.

The impression was reinforced when, at the age of twenty, he arrived in the papal city, to find himself surrounded by the Roman Classicism of Bramante, Michelangelo, Raphael and Peruzzi. That great inspirer Bramante enjoyed a high reputation for his own buildings as well: in particular, his work on St Peter's. Tradition ascribes the excellent

Palazzo della Cancelleria to him, but this has never been fully con-firmed. The beautiful *cortile* is perhaps his work. The work of Michelangelo as an architect in Florence has been referred to elsewhere in this book; here let me merely recall his major works in Rome: the reconstruction and continuation of St Peter's and the design of its magnificent dome, the redesigning of the Capitol square with its three palaces, familiar to every visitor to Rome, and finally his dignified and vigorous Porta Pia.

While still barely thirty, Vasari had the good fortune to meet the important artists who had transferred the Roman style to a Venetian setting, and to become friendly with the greatest of them. Iacopo Tatti, called Sansovino, had advanced to a prominent position in Venice after his flight during the sack of Rome. Two years later the *Signoria* had appointed him official architect to the republic. He created his first masterpiece in the Old Library, which stands on the southern side of St Mark's Square, still giving it an air of distinction. Michele San-micheli, a pupil of Bramante and a supporter of the ideas of Vitruvius and Roman proportions, was admired in Venice and other cities of the Veneto for the virile strength of his work. The third of these great architects, Andrea Palladio, combined features of Michele's gravity with his own easy elegance in highly esteemed palaces and villas; visitors to Venice will recall his remarkable church of San Giorgio Maggiore with its rich interior.

Equipped with impressions of works by the most eminent masters of the fruitful sixteenth century, Vasari in the years following his return from Venice began to translate his knowledge into practical achieve-ment. While working on the Villa Giulia he had to co-operate more or less voluntarily with Ammannati and Vignola, as previously men-tioned; but in fact they shared his views on architecture. Without them, he carried out a successful and admired work for Bindo Altoviti, a *Vigna*, which survived until 1870 when it was destroyed during the siege of Rome. Vasari must already have acquired a reputation as an architect, because he was invited by the Pope to take part in a closed competition for a large cornice for the Palazzo Farnese, along with prominent architects who included Michelangelo, the eventual winner. Vasari's work in Florence and other Tuscan cities, where he drew on his experience in Venice, has already been referred to.

The fact that Vasari was a better architect than he was a painter was due, in all probability, both to his character and to the circumstances. His unquestionable abilities in planning, organization, and clear, energetic direction of the working processes harmonized well with the demands of architecture; and since in this art he had constantly before him undistracted, the best, safest, and most original models, he found a school for life in this sphere.

Vasari's sober vitality, as well as his speed in large-scale enterprises, reveal a conscious dependability, combined with a sense of proportion and – generally speaking – a genuine distinction, whose results a later age must also acknowledge.

CHAPTER IV

The Most Eminent Painters . . .

LET US return to the work which nowadays constitutes the pivot of Vasari's production, his *Lives*. 'In this work,' Adolfo Venturi has said, 'he bestowed upon us his grandest picture.' We cannot but agree that this picture will live on long after his panels have crumbled and his frescoes have distintegrated.

In its final form the *Lives of the Most Eminent Painters, Sculptors, and Architects . . .* contains 108 biographies, and if to these we add the artists who are discussed in groups we get in all 250 painters, sculptors, architects, engravers, goldsmiths, and workers in stained glass. It is impossible to draw a sharp line of distinction between the various arts, since most of the artists dealt with were active in several fields, many of them, as was the custom, being at once painter, sculptor and architect.

The work covers a period of 300 years, beginning with Cimabue and including in the final part Michelangelo, other contemporary artists, and lastly Vasari himself. Painters form by far the biggest group and, as already stated, the present book is confined to these.

After a general introduction entitled *I tre Arti del Disegno* ('The three arts of design'), which sketches the origin, history, materials and techniques of the arts, followed by a backward glance at the works of classical antiquity and the early Middle Ages, Vasari goes on to the *Lives*. He deals with artists from over thirty parts of Italy, ranging from Lombardy to Venice and Sicily. No fewer than eighty-four are Florentines, the Sienese and Venetians coming next with fifteen each. Rome is represented by a modest two. The biographies vary in length from a few octavo pages to nearly 200, the space being by no means always apportioned according to artistic importance. As could be expected, the work of Michelangelo receives the fullest treatment, filling a whole book of some 200 pages. Vasari devotes a fair amount of space to himself, his autobiography, with which he concludes the work, taking up nearly seventy pages.

Much more important than the bulk, of course, is the subject matter. Having once begun, Vasari became fascinated by the material and could not content himself with a mere cataloguing; his temperament, his knowledge, and his genuine feeling for art impelled him to study, as well as he was able, the background, origins, training and styles of his artists. He had possessed since his youth an instinctive eye for what was new or great wherever he encountered it. His discussion of the artists of the Duecento and Trecento shows that, though he and his contemporaries had different ideas about the aims, form and style of painting he saw the period as the beginning of a new and significant epoch in pictorial art. To Vasari we owe a great many accounts – though some were taken from predecessors and some were merely legendary – of the ideas, characters, lives and careers of these early artists, material which, but for him, would long since have been lost.

He admits us to a motley world; a multitude of careers and achievements, in rough passage and in smooth, in light and shade. Few people today will want to read the whole of this material; many of the works mentioned seem to us unimportant; many names have little meaning for us. But the reader who seeks deliberately will be rewarded for his trouble by meeting a host of outstanding artists, introduced by a pioneer biographer.

In the following I shall try to extract from Vasari's text passages characteristic of his method and illustrative of the circumstances to which he ascribes importance in the world of art. To a large extent they will inevitably be fragmentary and anecdotal, in his own chosen manner, and as already exemplified above; but with the purely factual material his selection, the personal features which he emphasizes, and the theoretical and moral views which he propounds will convey an understanding of his character as an author. It will be necessary, if only for reasons of space, to restrict the number of examples and confine them mainly to artists of his own period: painters with whom he was personally acquainted or on terms of friendship.

As already stated, Vasari ascribes the beginnings of Italian painting to the 'primitives' of Florence and Siena – to Cimabue, Giotto, Duccio, and their pupils – and it is to his credit, more than to that of anyone else, that these early painters have obtained their rightful place in art history. He regarded them as the founders of the great advance which took place in the art of painting in the following centuries. He sees how essential they were to his whole view of art, realizing that without them neither he nor any of his contemporaries would have attained to such heights as he considers the sixteenth century to be.

Writing of Giovanni Cimabue, born in 1240, he says: 'He was the first for a thousand years to paint figures from nature . . . the first to paint on a panel (*su tavola*). Apprenticed to Greek (*i.e.* Byzantine) painters working at the time in Florence, he 'far excelled his masters, both in design and colour'. Vasari draws particular attention to a magnificent altarpiece showing the Madonna flanked by worshipping angels, which is now in the Uffizi, and he also praises Cimabue's fresco decorations in the church of St Francis at Assisi. These have now mostly disintegrated, but one – a Madonna and Child surrounded by angels and St Francis, in the lower church at Assisi – is quite well preserved, and is proof without further evidence that the Byzantine style was ebbing out.

plate 29
p. 77

Vasari quotes the popular legend about Cimabue, of how, walking near Florence, he met a shepherd boy sitting on a rock, drawing with obvious talent his father's sheep. Cimabue talked to him, and going home with him persuaded his father to allow him to take the boy as his apprentice. The boy who thus entered the world of art, which he was to influence for centuries, was Giotto di Bondone, born in 1266.

Vasari admires the masterpiece of Giotto's youth, the long series in the upper church of St Francis, which he later continued in the lower church, of stories illustrating the life of the saint; he dwells with pleasure on his beautiful Madonna, now in the Uffizi, and on the largescale masterpieces of his maturity in the church of S. Croce in Florence and the Arena chapel at Padua.

plate 38
p. 106

Although Siena in those distant days was a rival of Florence, Vasari recognizes that important developments were also taking place in the latter city towards the end of the Middle Ages. Here there arose a hither-to unknown painter, Duccio (Bernarduccio?) di Buoninsegna (born about 1250), who, as Vasari says, 'became a very famous painter, active in many cities'. Greeting him as an innovator in painting, he singles out, though he never actually saw it, his celebrated altarpiece, '*La Maestà*' ('The Queen of Heaven'), painted in 1308–11 for the cathedral at Siena. The altarpiece, radiant in gold and colour, is now in the Cathedral Museum at Siena.

plate 36
p. 105

'Nothing is known of Duccio's pupils,' Vasari says. But he is full of admiration for the charm and subtle invention of the painters who followed in Duccio's footsteps, such as Simone Martini, and he especially praises Simone's great fresco in Siena Town Hall, called, like Duccio's, '*La Maestà*'.

plate 28
p. 77

Pietro Lorenzetti, whom Vasari calls Laurati (being unaware that he was a brother of Ambrogio), was 'an admirable painter, who worked with real mastery'. Ambrogio, he says, 'possessed a very fine, rich power of expression', exemplified, among other works, in a series of frescoes called 'Good and Bad Government', in Siena Town Hall.

plate 37
p. 106

Vasari discusses many Italian painters who perpetuated the spirit and the work of the primitive masters, absorbing elements both from Florence and from the Siena group, and whose works are greatly esteemed today. Among others, he touches on Giottino, otherwise known as Giotto di Maestro Stefano. 'Learning from his father', he says, 'the rudiments of the art . . . he continued in the manner of Giotto, and so well did he succeed in this that he was generally known as "Giottino" ("the little Giotto"), many wrongly believing him to be a son of Giotto.' Giottino left a superbly composed altarpiece, luminous in colour, now in the Uffizi. Another of the artists dealt with in this group is Andrea Orcagna, the creator or inspirer of the moving 'Triumph of Death' in the historic cemetery of the Camposanto in Pisa. The authorship of this fresco is now disputed, most art historians being inclined to think that it was done by Orcagna's pupil Francesco Traini.

Simone Martini   Ambrogio Lorenzetti

In following the progressive course of Vasari's *Lives* we may pause with him in the Quattrocento, the fifteenth century. A hundred years after Giotto, we arrive at another turning-point in the history of painting, a time when a star of the first magnitude rose in the sky of Florence – Masaccio. The name was given, as a satirical nickname, to Tomaso di Ser Guidi, who was born in 1401 at San Giovanni, a village in the Arno valley in the province of Arezzo. For this young genius – only twenty-seven when he died – Vasari is full of praise.

'Masaccio, he says, 'was a humble, friendly, quiet-spoken, contemplative person, indifferent to clothes, food, and other worldly goods; hard-working and co-operative, he never collected fees due to him except when in great need.' Some outstanding pictures by this artist have survived, the best known being his major work, the decoration in fresco of a chapel in the church of S. Maria del Carmine in Florence, which was paid for and dedicated by Antonio Brancacci, diplomatist and silk merchant, whose name it bears. 'The admirable Masaccio', writes

plate 39
p. 107

Vasari, 'exalted in every respect the manner of Giotto . . . going so far by ceaseless study that he must be ranked among the first to have prevailed over the resistance, the imperfections, and the difficulties of the art. . . . He required of art that it should have simplicity of design and colour, agreeing in flesh tints and costumes with living objects in nature. . . . He introduced beautiful poses, movement, life, form, and vitality into his figures. He strove to give expression to the finest thoughts and feelings in the spirit of nature, as well as individuality of physical appearance.' Vasari goes on to say that Leonardo, Raphael, Botticelli, Michelangelo, and many another among the greatest of the Renaissance painters sat day after day in the Brancacci chapel sketching from Masaccio's figures.

From the rich Quattrocento Vasari singles out Paolo Uccello and Piero della Francesca, who besides their achievement in painting carried out fundamental work on the theory of perspective.

He dwells warmly on the sympathetic Fra Angelico, 'the angelic brother', admired and loved in all Italy, and also known by his monastic name of Fra Giovanni of Fiesole.

As a layman, he could easily have lived by his art and earned good money, but for his soul's sake he resolved to enter the Dominican Order. . . . Would that all priests led lives like this truly angelic father, serving God and their neighbours. . . . He was lovable, unselfish, never irritable with his brothers. . . . He was always extremely devout in his painting, his saints being more like saints than those of other painters. . . . He never took up his brush without offering a prayer, and he could never paint a Crucifixion without shedding tears. . . . Such great and exceptional ability as Fra Giovanni's could only develop in a man of the most pious conduct; for those artists who wish to create religious and sacred works must themselves be religious and devout. But when works depicting *nude* figures are created by men weak in faith and respect for religion they arouse carnal desires and lascivious lusts. Wherefore one censures such works for their lack of morality and praises them for their technique. Yet I

plate 40
p. 108

31–33 *Three examples of Vasari's work as an architect.* Above: *The Villa Giulia, Rome (in collaboration with Vignola and Ammannati).* Centre: *chapel of the Palazzo dei Cavalieri, Pisa; the walls, decorated with monochrome frescoes by Vasari, are hung with captured Turkish banners.* Below: *Palazzo dei Cavalieri, Pisa* (see p. 74).

34 Giotto: Madonna and Child with angels.

do not wish to suggest – wrongly – that what is awkward and clumsy should be deemed sacred and the fine and good work lascivious, as some do when, seeing figures of women and youths rather more beautiful or more charming and graceful than usual, they at once regard them as indecent. However, I would have no one believe that I approve of the painting of practically nude figures in churches, for they demonstrate that the artist has failed to entertain a proper respect for the place.

Vasari introduced his account of Leonardo da Vinci with words which bear the moralizing impress of Annibale Caro:

The heavens often shower on men and women the richest of gifts, and sometimes they do so with such supernatural and lavish abundance as to bestow upon a single individual beauty, grace, as well as talent, so that whatever he may do his every action is so divine that he outstrips all other men, manifesting his genius as a gift of God rather than a human acquirement. All men have seen this to be so in Leonardo da Vinci; for besides a physical beauty never sufficiently extolled he displayed divine gifts in everything that he did, his genius being so great . . . that whatever the difficulties of the enterprises to which he turned his hand he solved them with ease, for he possessed great physical strength combined with agility and a courage always royal and magnanimous. . . .

*plate 49
p. 145*

Leonardo practised not one art but all of those that are dependent upon design, and he had great talent for geometry besides being very musical, playing the lute with great ability and being excellent in the art of improvisation. . . . In entertaining, Leonardo was so pleasant that he won every man's heart. Although he may well be said to have owned nothing and to have worked little, he always kept a servant as well as horses. . . .

After describing in detail the master's principal work, 'The Last Supper' in the refectory of S. Maria delle Grazie in Milan, Vasari tells the following story as characteristic of Leonardo: 'There were still two heads to be done, that of Christ, which he would not look for on earth, feeling unable to conceive the beauty and celestial grace that must have been incarnate in the divinity, and that of Judas . . . for whom he did not think he could find a better head that that of the importunate and tactless prior . . .! The head of Christ remained unfinished. The sublimity of this painting, both in its composition and the care with which it was executed, induced in King Louis XII of France an ardent desire to take it home with him. Accordingly, he sought by all means to find an architect who would frame it in wood and iron, so that it might be transported regardless of the cost. But the king was thwarted in his desire, as the picture was painted on the wall, and so had to remain with the Milanese.'

Vasari regrets – as do all later connoisseurs – that Leonardo's all-embracing and restless spirit did not give him time and opportunity to leave behind him more paintings than he did. 'We see,' he writes, 'how Leonardo, full of knowledge of art, commenced many things and finished none; for it seemed to him that his hand could never attain to the artistic perfection which he believed that he saw in things, his mind forming such subtle and extraordinary difficulties that they could never find expression through the most perfect hands. And his ideas caused him to philosophize over the natural sciences, seeking to understand the properties of plants and ever studying the motions of the firmament, the revolutions of the moon, and the course of the sun.'

In the Quattrocento there emerged from the private 'academy' in Padua of Iacopo Squarcione (a mediocre painter but an inspiring teacher) one of the greatest geniuses in Italian painting – Andrea Mantegna. Prompted once more by Annibale Caro, Vasari writes in the introduction to his account of him in the *Lives*:

Those who work with skill for which they are rewarded are aware of the renewed strength given by encouragement; for men who expect honour and reward are insensible to toil and fatigue. True, skill does not always meet with the recognition and reward that were accorded to Andrea Mantegna, who though he was born of humble stock and as a child tended cattle, yet by good fortune and his talents

Piero della Francesca   *Masaccio*

rose to the rank of knight. . . . For the Duke he painted Ludovico
Gonzaga and his family, as well as a 'Triumph of Caesar' which is
the best thing that he ever did. . . . The plane on which the figures
stood was set higher than the point of view; and while placing the
feet of those in the foreground on the front profile of the plane, he
allowed the others, that were farther back, to diminish, removing the
feet and legs from view as required by the logic of the viewpoint. . . .
This whole work could not be more beautiful or better designed.

plate 43
p. 117

These paintings, forming a frieze 90 feet long, are now at Hampton
Court Palace, near London.

A painter highly esteemed by modern connoisseurs of Italian art is
Piero della Francesca, born *c.* 1416. He was also admired in Vasari's
day, as one of those Italian geniuses – not uncommon – who combined
distinguished art with outstanding theoretical studies. His works in the
church of San Francesco at Arezzo were some of the first with which

the boy Giorgio became acquainted. Writing of Piero's great fresco cycle, 'The Legend of the Cross', Vasari says:

> He painted the story beginning with the sons of Adam, who, when they buried their father, sowed under his tongue the seed that grew into the tree from which Christ's cross was taken; and ending in the erection of the cross by the Emperor Heraclius, who walks bare-foot through Jerusalem bearing it on his shoulder. . . . We see, for example, the costumes of the Queen of Sheba's women, done in a wonderful new style; and many scenes from olden times, full of life . . . such as a peasant who stands with his hands resting on a shovel, listening to St Helen while the three crosses are being dug up – none of which could be painted better. . . . He also painted a group of horses, so skilfully foreshortened that they may almost be called – in the light of the times – *too* beautiful.

The virile art of Piero della Francesca, which ranks him with Mantegna, still testifies to his exquisite feeling and sense of plastic form.

A pupil of Piero della Francesca, and inheritor of his austere, dramatic art, whom we meet in the latter half of the fifteenth century, is Luca Signorelli. It was he who started Vasari off on his artistic career in the early days at Arezzo, an engaging master whom he always recalled with the greatest veneration.

> Luca [he says] was famous in his day throughout Italy, and his works were esteemed above all others; for in those creations he demonstrated the rendering of nudes, and how it is possible, by art and skill, to make them seem alive. . . . In the church of the Madonna, the cathedral of Orvieto, he completed the chapel begun by Fra Giovanni, with scenes of the end of the world.

plate 44
p. 118

> In the chapel he depicted everything at the Day of Judgment with singularly imaginative invention: angels, demons, upheavals, earthquakes, the 'miracles of anti-Christ', and many beautiful figures, bringing to life the horror that will prevail on that dreadful day. In doing so he gave heart to all those who have come after him,

Fra Angelico   *Fra Filippo Lippi*

whereby they have found the difficulties of this style but small. . . .

Luca was a man of the best manners, honest and amiable in friendship, in conversation charming, friendly to everyone, above all obliging to anyone who required his work, while being lively and communicative in his teaching.

Another monk, Fra Filippo Lippi, of Florence, won fame at about the same time as Angelico. Besides this artist's rich and versatile artistic achievement, Vasari describes his unusual career, giving such a vivid and colourful picture both of Fra Filippo's life and experiences, and of the background of the early Renaissance, that we must quote him. Left an orphan at the age of two, Filippo, who had been born in Florence in 1406, was lodged with an aunt, who endeavoured to educate him. Unable to cope with the intelligent and undisciplined boy, she placed him, at the age of eight, in the monastery of the Carmine, to become a monk.

Here he proved to be as skilful and inventive in mechanical things as he was inapt and indolent in learning the sciences. . . . In class he spent all his time scrawling faces and caricatures in his books and those of his fellows. The prior therefore resolved to provide him with every opportunity to study painting. The Carmine chapel was being decorated at that time by Masaccio, and Filippo was delighted with it, finding it very beautiful. He therefore paid daily visits to it, constantly practising with many young men who were always sketching there. . . . While still young and immature he created such praiseworthy works that they were to be marvelled at. . . . He made rapid progress, and had soon acquired the style of Masaccio to such perfection that his pictures became more and more like the master's, and many people said the spirit of Masaccio had descended to Filippo.

It must have been a lively and fascinating sight to see the budding painters, aged sixteen to seventeen, flocking round this young genius of twenty-three or four.

plate 41
p. 108

Filippo's later, more individual works radiate a singular charm and poetry, supported by splendid colour and combining, it may truly be said, something of Fra Angelico's delicacy with the vigour of Masaccio.

Filippo painted for the elder Cosimo some pictures which were presented to Pope Eugenius IV, and which brought him into favour with the latter. 'It is said', Vasari relates,

that Filippo was so amorous that whenever he saw a woman who pleased him he was ready to give all he possessed in order to win her; and if unable to attain this end he had at least to paint her, cooling his ardour with work and words. When in such a mood as this he would find it hard to control himself, and would care little or nothing for the work in hand. So once, when he had commissioned him for some work in his house, Cosimo locked him in, in order that he might not waste any of his time outside. After two days of this, Filippo was so overcome by amorous desires and passions that in the evening he cut up his sheet with scissors, let himself down from the

Luca Signorelli   Andrea del Castagno

window with it, and devoted several days to his pleasures. When he was missed, Cosimo ordered a search to be made, and he was finally escorted back to his work. From that time on Cosimo allowed him to come and go as he liked, regretting that he had locked him in, and reflecting on his amorous folly and the danger it exposed him to. Thereafter, Cosimo always sought to keep him to his work by friendly means, and was served with all the greater readiness, so much so that he would say that geniuses are gifts from Heaven, not pack-asses. . .

Once when in the region of Ancona Filippo went for a sail in a boat, together with some friends. There they were captured by Moors, whose galleys scoured those parts, and carried off to Barbary, to be put in chains and treated as slaves. He remained there for eighteen months, and endured great hardships. Then one day it occurred to him to draw a portrait of his master, whom he had often seen. So taking a piece of charcoal from the fire he drew him in full figure in his Moorish dress, on a white wall. The other slaves, to whom this seemed a miracle, drawing and painting being in those parts unknown, reported the matter to their master, and in consequence he was liberated from the chains he had long borne. Great indeed is the force of art when it leads one who has the power to punish and condemn into doing the opposite, granting friendship and freedom instead of punishment and death. After doing some paintings for his master, Filippo was delivered in safety to Naples. . . .

The nuns of S. Margherita entrusted him with the painting of a panel for their high altar; and while at work on it one day he observed the daughter of Francesco Buti, a Florentine citizen, who was being educated as a nun. Gazing at Lucrezia – for such was her name – Filippo found her graceful and beautiful. By favour of the nuns he obtained permission to paint her, and to use her picture in his works as the Madonna. When doing so he fell even deeper in love with her, and finally found means of abducting her from the nunnery. . . . The nuns felt greatly ashamed at this, and her father was never happy again. He tried every means of inducing her to return, but whether from fear or some other reason, she refused. So she remained with Filippo, and bore him a son who was also named Filippo, and who like his father became an excellent and celebrated painter.

In order to distinguish him from his father, the son was later known as Filippino. The father is said to have married his beloved without waiting for the dispensation which the Pope was very willing to grant, though the latest opinion seems to be that he did not marry her, even after getting the dispensation. The princes of the Church would appear to have been extremely forthcoming in the granting of special favours as a return for the friendship of famous artists.

The source of Vasari's story about Filippo's capture by the Moors is unknown and the story is unsubstantiated; whether he believed it or not, it must have seemed too good to withhold.

Filippo's most gifted pupil was Alessandro, 'called according to our custom', Vasari says, 'Sandro'. His surname was Filipepi, but his

35 *Pietro Lorenzetti: Madonna and Child with St Francis and St John the Evangelist.*

36 *Duccio: Madonna and Child. Detail from 'La Maestà'.*

37 *Ambrogio Lorenzetti: detail from 'The Good Reign and the Bad Reign'. 'An admirable painter,' says Vasari, 'who worked with real mastery'.*

38 *Giotto: The Death of St Francis of Assisi.*

39 Masaccio: *The Apostles Peter and John distributing alms.*

40 Fra Angelico: Crucifixion (detail, showing a group of saints at the foot of the Cross). 'He never took up his brush without offering a prayer, and he could never paint a crucifixion without shedding tears.'

41 Filippo Lippi: Madonna and Child.

better-known name, Botticelli, he took from his godfather, a goldsmith. Having earned a good deal of money in his youth by talented work in Rome, where he had been summoned by the Pope to paint frescoes in the Sistine Chapel, he had soon squandered it by loose and reckless living.

> Given to brooding, he annotated and illustrated some of Dante's works. . . . Besides some circular pictures, he painted in various Florentine houses a fair number of female figures, more or less in the nude, two of these being still in the Castello, Duke Cosimo's villa. One of them represents the birth of Venus, who with cupids is being wafted ashore by the gods of the air and the wind; while the other is a Venus who is being adorned by the Graces with flowers to proclaim the spring. As will be seen, he has depicted them with great charm. . . . [They are now in the Uffizi.]
>
> Sandro painted so beautifully that after his death artists went to great trouble in order to obtain sketches by him. I have some in my own collection that were done with great skill and genius.

plate 45
p. 118

During his stay in Venice Vasari was much impressed by the beauty which that city had bequeathed to painting, and does not omit to say that the new school was inspired by the spirit of Florence, as brought home from Tuscany by Iacopo Bellini. Of this painter, and his admirable sons, he says:

'What is founded in genius will eventually rise upward, though the origin may in many ways seem base and insignificant, and will continue until it attains to the peak of fame – a fact which can be plainly seen from the humble beginnings of the house of Bellini and the status which it has achieved through painting.'

Iacopo Bellini, who was born about 1400, became a pupil of Gentile da Fabriano in Tuscany, but it was not until he had taken up permanent residence in Venice that, as Vasari says,

> he grew in esteem and fame, becoming one of the greatest and most highly regarded men in his art, and ensured that the renown he

acquired in painting was not only preserved but advanced and in, creased; he had two sons who were both devoted to art and greatly gifted, the one being Giovanni and the other Gentile. . . . Now, as these two sons grew up, Iacopo taught them with all diligence and care the basis of the art. But before long they had both surpassed their father, who – happy in the knowledge of this – ever encouraged them to excel one another, desiring them to achieve fame like the Tuscans. . . .

plate 52
p. 146
As painters nearly always do in that city they painted on canvas, unlike those elsewhere who use panels of common and white poplar. These two trees mostly grow on the banks of rivers and lakes, and produce wood quite soft and excellent to paint on, binding well when treated with mastic. In Venice, however, they do not paint pictures on panels, or, if they do, they use only spruce, which the city has in abundance, importing large quantities from Germany down the Adige as well as some supplies from Dalmatia. As I have said, it is common in Venice to paint on canvas, because it does not split like wood nor does it become worm,eaten; moreover, on canvas it is possible to paint pictures of any desired size, which can then conveniently be sent, at small cost, wherever one chooses. . . .

Though they made themselves equally independent, to live and to work each for himself, they yet had so great respect one for another, and the sons for the father, that each praised one another and dis, paraged himself, the one seeking to excel the other in humility, and not less in goodness and courtesy than in the excellence of their art.

At a time when Florence had achieved great fame through the works of Leonardo there was a citizen of Venice who attained to no mean glory by his talent and excellence, far surpassing the so highly esteemed Bellinis and everyone else who painted in the city at that time. This man was Giorgio Zorzi, who was born at Castelfranco in 1478. The name Giorgione was given to him because of his stature and the greatness of his mind. Though he was of very humble origin, his manners were gentle and polished all his life, and he was

Raphael   *Andrea del Sarto*

fond of all kinds of music and amorous affairs, being indeed famous for his divine playing of the lute, so that he was invited to perform at the concerts and festivals given by the nobility.

Anticipating the high opinion held of Giorgione later, Vasari observes: 'It must be said that he was born to endow his figures with both spirit and flesh tints better than any other man then painting, not only in Venice but anywhere.' A great many works have been ascribed to Giorgione in after-years, but very few are now thought to be authentic. Among the best known are 'A Knight of Malta' in the Uffizi, 'The Three Philosophers' in Vienna, and 'The Tempest', in Venice.

plate 53
p. 147

Tintoretto (Iacopo Robusti) was, like Giorgione, a Renaissance figure entirely after Vasari's heart.

He was versed in many arts, such as the playing of instruments, but in painting he was extraordinarily original, rapid and resolute – the finest brain that painting has ever known. . . . He would have been one of the greatest painters Venice has known, if only he had been conscious of the great gifts Nature had bestowed upon him and had developed them by study and concentration and not dashed off his work as he did, as if desirous of proving that this art may be taken as a jest. Often he would leave his works in the form of rough sketches instead of completing them, so that one sees the brush strokes as though placed by chance instead of with design and forethought.

Since the painters just referred to had left newly completed works which Vasari could constantly refer to, and since it was his good fortune, as he tells us, to meet great artists, see their works with his own eyes, and listen to their advice and counsel with his own ears, it is not surprising that his pen should be inspired.

Vasari knew Andrea del Sarto long enough to be dominated by admiration and affection for him all his life.

plate 47
p. 135
plate 56
p. 148

In Andrea [he says] one sees a revelation of nature and art, all that painting is capable of in design, colour and invention, and in such great measure that had Andrea but been bolder and more vigorous in spirit, as he was a man of the greatest genius and profound judgment in this art, he would doubtless have been unequalled; but a certain timidity, reserve and restraint would never allow in him that vital glow and vigour which, with his other qualities, would have made him a truly divine painter. Yet his figures are flawless and in every respect perfect. Andrea's works as well as his name will live in the remote future, and my present publication will preserve the memory of them, I trust, for centuries to come.

Raphael, who had died in 1520 before Vasari had arrived at manhood, he regarded as a superhuman figure in the world of art. Oral statements by pupils and others who had been closely associated with Raphael, recorded memoirs, letters, and above all the works themselves, left deep impressions on Vasari's mind. 'Raphael', he says, 'possessed

Sandro Botticelli   *Iacopo Pontormo*

goodness, modesty, great charm, industry, beauty, and admirable ways
. . . . not merely a man, but a "mortal God".'

Interwoven in his glowing account of Raphael's works, Vasari gives
us a vivid portrait of this prince of art: 'Everyone courted Raphael's
favour; he was given the greatest commissions in the Vatican and St
Peter's, and he was sought after by innumerable pupils and assistants. . . .
When attending a festive event he would arrive from his *palazzo* in
the Borgo with an escort of anything up to fifty pupils. . . . And wishing
to know all about European art, he despatched draughtsmen with
instructions to send pictures home from all parts of Italy and Greece. . . .'

One of his most admired productions, entirely his own work, is the
'Galatea' which he painted about 1514, and which adorns a salon
adjoining the great hall of the Farnesina in Rome. The goddess is
shown being drawn across the sea by dolphins, surrounded by cupids,
tritons and nymphs, the whole scene radiating intense vitality, delight,
beauty, and sweetness.

Writing of a turning-point in Raphael's painting, Vasari says:

By this time he had achieved great fame in Rome, but, though he possessed a noble and beautiful style which commanded universal admiration, and though he had tirelessly studied many classical works in that city, he had previously failed to embody in his figures that grandeur and majesty which he gave to them from now on. It came about that at this time Michelangelo, while working on the (Sistine) Chapel, became involved in a dispute with the Pope . . . and for that reason had to flee to Florence. On this occasion Bramante, who held the key to the chapel, allowed his close friend Raphael to inspect it, in order that he might acquire Michelangelo's style and manner. As a result, Raphael, who had completed his picture of the prophet Isaiah in S. Agostino in Rome, immediately repainted it, improving his style beyond measure and investing it with greater majesty. When he saw this work, Michelangelo declared that it was Bramante who had done him 'this injury'.

plate 48
p. 136

Raphael's fame had also spread to France and Flanders, and the German painter Albrecht Dürer, a quite remarkable painter and the creator of the finest copper engravings, paid Raphael the tribute of sending him his own portrait, painted in water-colours on cambric. This material allowed the light to pass through on both sides – without the use of white paint – and was only toned and modelled with water-colours, the highlights being formed by the white colouring of the fabric itself. This seemed marvellous to Raphael; and in return he sent Albrecht many drawings, which the latter greatly prized. . . .

Raphael was an amorous man, very fond of women. . . . Consequently, in the matter of sensual pleasures his friends made certain allowances for him, perhaps more than was proper. When, for example, his friend Agostino Chigi employed him to paint the first loggia in his palace, Raphael, because of his love for a young woman, was unable to do much work. Agostino, in despair, arranged that Raphael's mistress should stay in the part of the house where he was employed; and so the work was completed. . . .

Leonardo da Vinci   *Giovanni Bellini*

His close friend Cardinal Bibbiena had for many years urged Raphael to marry. While not expressly refusing, Raphael kept the matter open for three or four years. Pressed by the Cardinal again after the lapse of this time, he felt bound by his word and consented to marry Maria Bibbiena, the Cardinal's niece. But still he kept on putting the matter off, and the marriage never took place. . . . Once, following a period of exceptional dissipation, Raphael fell into a very violent fever. Feeling his strength failing him and death draw⁄ ing near, like a good Christian he sent his mistress from the house and then left her enough to live on in a manner fitting to her station.

A living bond linked Vasari to the life of Raphael: his personal friendship with Giulio Romano, Raphael's most talented pupil and heir. Vasari thought him almost Raphael's counterpart: '. . . entertaining, pleasant, charming, delightful, and admirable in all his ways. Of

Raphael's pupils none followed him more faithfully than Giulio – in invention, style, design, and colour. None was more thorough, bolder, more assured, more individual, or richer than he . . . he could do everything!' Giulio assisted Raphael in the work on the papal loggias and painted large parts of the oil and fresco pictures under Raphael's direction. He drew the architecture in numerous pictures by the master and completed his unfinished works after his death. Giulio Romano seems to later beholders a versatile and competent painter, and is also one of the progenitors of Mannerism.

During his stay in Venice in 1542, as described above, Vasari got on very friendly terms with Titian – Tiziano Vecellio da Cadore – then about sixty-three and in his best years. Vasari studied Titian's works in Venice and many other cities: the great church pictures and his vast works in the palace of the Doges (many of which were lost in the great fire of 1577), among them portraits of the Doges. He saw the many portraits of princely personages, Popes and cardinals, and he has the strongest words of praise for Titian's beautiful women: Flora, Danaë, Venus, and the 'Sacred and Profane Love'.

When Titian, summoned by Cardinal Farnese, came in 1546 to Rome, where Vasari happened to be staying, the latter took friendly care of him, showing him the sights of the city and introducing him to his many friends, among them Michelangelo. 'Titian', Vasari says, 'is a very able and competent painter, like scarcely any other of his profession; from Heaven he has received nothing but favour and fortune. Every prince and prominent person who has visited Venice has called upon him at his house. . . . Titian has created works which deserve everlasting praise. . . . They will live for as long as the memory of famous men endures. He deserves to be called the greatest master of our day for his imitation of natural tints; a foundation of good draughtsmanship would have placed him alongside Raphael and Michelangelo.'

plate 54
p. 147

This faint praise seems to have been Michelangelo's also. 'When Michelangelo and Vasari', says the latter, 'went one day to the Belvedere in the Vatican in order to pay their respects to Titian, who had been

42 *Piero della Francesca: The Queen of Sheba, from the great fresco cycle, 'The Legend of the Cross'.*

43 *Mantegna: Ludovico Gonzaga and his family.*

44 Luca Signorelli:
detail from 'The Damned' (see p. 100).

45 Botticelli: The Birth of Venus.

given a residence there, they saw, just completed, a painting of a female nude' – now in the Museo Nazionale, Pinacoteca, Naples – 'supposed to represent Danaë with Jupiter in the form of golden rain in her lap. They praised it warmly, as one does in the presence of the artist. When they were discussing the painting together as they left, Michelangelo spoke warmly of Titian, saying that he thought highly of his colour and his style, but adding that it was a pity the Venetians had not first learnt how to draw.'

Little could these two friends suspect that a time would come when the worship of colour would reduce design to amorphous strokes or geometrical elements – and indeed that the purely subjective experiences, emotions, and more or less conscious and recollected dreams of painters would find expression on canvases which could be coveted by collectors.

Vasari met many other distinguished painters in Rome at that time. One who particularly appealed to him was Sebastiano Luciani (born in 1485), who is best known under the name of Sebastiano del Piombo. His Venetian delight in colour, his psychologically subtle and penetrating portraiture, his *chiaroscuro* (which appears to anticipate features in Rembrandt's style of painting), placed him in Vasari's opinion on a level with Raphael. His account of Sebastiano throws interesting light on the keen rivalry between design and colour in painting, and on the argument as to whether Raphael or Michelangelo took pride of place.

Not painting, but music, many say, was Sebastiano's first profession; for besides singing, he delighted in playing various instruments, especially the lute. . . . While still young he turned to painting, learning the elements from Giovanni Bellini, by then an old man. But Giorgione having introduced the more harmonious modern style, with glowing colours, Sebastiano left Giovanni and joined Giorgione, with whom he stayed so long that in great part he acquired the master's style. . . . Agostino Chigi, a rich merchant of Siena who had many business connections in Venice, hearing him greatly praised, invited him to Rome; for apart from his painting, he was much pleased that Sebastiano was so good at playing the lute and was pleasant and amiable company. . . .

Meanwhile, Raphael had become so famous that his friends said his paintings were superior to those of Michelangelo in colour, design and grace. . . . . Sebastiano, however, was not one of these, since he possessed fine judgment and fully appreciated the value of both. So for some time Michelangelo gave his heart to Sebastiano, because his colour and grace pleased him much, and took him under his protection, thinking that if he gave Sebastiano help in design in exchange for Sebastiano's help with colouring he might succeed in confounding his rival under cover of a third person.

Thereafter Sebastiano was given the commission for a picture in a chapel at Viterbo, a picture of the Madonna mourning the dead Christ.

Whereas the composition and the cartoon came from Michelangelo, the work was completed with great diligence by Sebastiano, who introduced a much-admired evening landscape, so that all who saw the work thought it very beautiful. . . .

Sebastiano painted many admirable portraits, among others of Andrea Doria [in the Palazzo Doria, Rome] and Pietro Aretino [presented by Aretino to his birthplace, Arezzo]. The latter is not only an excellent likeness but also a remarkable example of technical virtuosity, since it shows five or six different kinds of black – velvet, satin, silk, brocade, cloth, and finally a deep-black beard – so admirably rendered in the details that living nature could not do more. . . .

plate 55
p. 148

When Cardinal Ippolito de' Medici fell in love with Signora Giulia Gonzago, who was then living at Fondi, he sent Sebastiano, with an escort of four light horsemen, to paint her there. Sebastiano finished the portrait in a month, reproducing the celestial beauty of the lady; and the Cardinal perceived it to be far superior to any of Sebastiano's other works.

Sebastiano's appointment as keeper of the seal to the Pope, and what came of it, will be discussed later.

Michelangelo   *Titian*

Michelangelo Buonarroti (1475–1564) ruled the world of art for two-thirds of a century and was the object of Vasari's endless and unqualified adoration. 'The Ruler of Heaven', he says in the introduction to his life,

> . . . resolved to send down to the earth a genius universal in each art, to show single-handed the perfection of line and shadow, and who should give relief to his paintings, show a sound judgment in sculpture, and in architecture should render habitations convenient, safe, healthy, pleasant, well-proportioned, and enriched with various ornaments. He further endowed him with true moral philosophy and a sweet poetic spirit, so that the world should marvel at the singular eminence of his life and works and all his actions, seeming rather divine than earthly. . . . And seeing that in such skills, and especially in painting, sculpture, and architecture, the spirits of Tuscany stand ever ahead of others, God chose Florence for his home.

Michelangelo was the only contemporary artist still alive whom he included in the first edition of the *Lives*. Besides recording the artist's life, beginning with his apprenticeship to Domenico Ghirlandaio from the age of fourteen and his admission to the house of Lorenzo the Magnificent at the age of sixteen, down to the last bitter and arduous years in Rome, and describing all his works, Vasari gives many intimate details of the man himself.

Michelangelo was a good Christian; though rich, he lived unpretentiously, and not very sociably, by himself. He gave away many drawings and other works and generously supported the poor. His independence would not allow him to accept gifts from anyone. . . . In temperament he was rather short with those who offended him, but was never vindictive. His conversation was distinguished by weighty replies and original, entertaining and witty observations. . . . A friend who was a priest once said to him: 'It is a pity you have never taken a wife!' 'All too often,' Michelangelo replied, ' I have had to put up with a woman – art – that has always pestered me, and my children are the works I leave behind me.'

At this time Vasari was with him daily, and one morning the Pope decided, because of the Jubilee year, that they should receive a double indulgence if they would ride round to the 'seven churches'. In the course of their ride from one church to the other they had many valuable and objective conversations about art, which Vasari employed for a dialogue that on a suitable occasion will be published, together with other matters relating to art.

Unfortunately the dialogue has not survived.

When the first edition of the *Lives* had been printed in 1550 Vasari gave Michelangelo a copy of the work. 'My friend was very pleased with it,' he writes, 'and it was not long before Michelangelo, after reading the book, sent me a sonnet, written by himself, as a mark of his friendly regard.'

This sonnet was followed by a new one, and later by two others, written in the old master's rather shaky handwriting: 'I am sending you two sonnets, and though it is stuff and nonsense I do so that you may see

Sebastiano del Piombo   Giorgione

to what I have directed my thoughts; and when you reach the age of eighty-one you will believe me. . . .' The subsequent correspondence deals with one thing and another in an intimate and friendly tone. Michelangelo records his grief at the death of his servant Urbino, who had served him in loyalty and friendship for twenty-seven years and was to have been his support at the close of his own life. In another letter he expresses his pleasure at the birth of a son to his nephew Lionardo in Florence: '*Messer Giorgio, amico caro*, I have derived the greatest pleasure from your letter, from which I see that you remember this poor old man, and even more because you write that you have witnessed the triumph of the birth of a new Buonarroto; for this news I give you my best thanks. But this splendour does not please me; men should not laugh when all the world weeps. In short, it seems to me that Lionardo has displayed very poor judgment, especially in holding so large a feast for one who is born – a feast which should be reserved for the death of one who has lived well. . . .'

SONNET BY MICHELANGELO TO GIORGIO VASARI

for sending him 'Le Vite de' più eccellenti
Architetti Pittori et Scultori . . .'

1550

Se con lo stile ò coi colori avete
Alla natura pareggiato l'arte
Anzi a quella scemato il pregio in parte,
Che 'l bel di lei più bello a noi rendete;

Poi che con dotta man posto vi sete
A più degno lavoro, a vergar carte,
Quel che vi manca, a lei di pregio in parte
Nel dar vita ad altrui, tutto togliate.

Che se secolo alcuno omai contese
In far bell' opre, almen cedale, poi
Che convien ch'al prescritto fine arrive.

Or le memorie altrui, già spente, accese
Tornando, fate or che fien quelle e voi,
Malgrado d'essa, eternalmente vivi.

In another letter, Michelangelo informs his younger colleague of a major technical mishap during the work of building St Peter's, which caused a great stir. He describes, carefully illustrated by sketches, how an arch of a side chapel – the 'King of France's Chapel' – collapsed owing to errors made by one of the trusted master craftsmen in the construction of the centering, with the result that everything built on it had to be pulled down, causing many months of delay.

SONNET BY MICHELANGELO TO GIORGIO VASARI

On the Lives of the Painters

With pencil and with palette hitherto
you made your art high Nature's paragon;
nay more, from Nature her own prize you won,
making what she made fair more fair to view.

Now that your learnèd hand with labour new
of pen and ink a worthier work hath done,
what erst you lacked, what still remained her own,
the power of giving life, is gained for you.

If man in any age with Nature vied
in beauteous workmanship, they had to yield
when to the fated end years brought their name.

You, reilluming memories that died,
in spite of Time and Nature have revealed
for them and for yourself eternal fame.

(Translation by J. A. Symonds)

Since 1534, Michelangelo had kept away from Florence (being unable to trust the Medici), and worked almost entirely in Rome. After completing the 'Last Judgment' in the Sistine Chapel, he had devoted himself primarily to architecture; after the completion of the Palazzo Farnese and the conversion of the Capitol square, he had concentrated every effort on the continuation of St Peter's. In those years, when his fame was at its highest, Duke Cosimo tried hard to induce the master to

plate 50
p. 145

return to Florence, in order, among other things, to complete the frontage – still incomplete to this day – of the church of San Lorenzo, using as his spokesman, in most cases, his ever-willing adviser Vasari. In letters which the latter wrote on the Duke's behalf, Florence and the life that was lived there are depicted in a rosy light and glittering promises are held out to persuade him to come. It is apparent from Michelangelo's replies that he still feels reluctant and mistrustful, and one senses his dislike of having to do menial work in Florence. Finally, he makes it clear that his artistic fortunes are definitively linked to Rome. In spite of the malevolence of envious cliques (especially the 'Sangallo gang') and trouble with the Pope, who was not always loyal and fair, his conscience bade him not to break faith at a time vital to the successful completion of the dome of St Peter's.

One or two quotations from the letters will suffice to show the tensions involved. Vasari writes: 'Flee from that "avaricious Babylon", like our fellow-citizen Petrarch, who, dejected by a like ingratitude, chose peace in Padua – as I promise you will achieve it in Florence. . . .' And later: '. . . and should anyone maliciously tell you that ignorance and terror prevail among people here, I will reply that in that case it is among those who do not love justice and peace and those who seek hatred and treachery right to the house of Satan; but those who tread the path of virtue and live under this prince's favour are also under the grace of God. . . .'

In one of his replies, dated 1555, Michelangelo says: 'I was forced to build St Peter's, and I have worked at it for eight years, not merely as a gift, but with the greatest tribulations and annoyances. If I were to go now, when there is help to be got and money to spend and I am vaulting the dome, it would mean ruin to this building project, disgrace me in the eyes of all Christendom, and be a very great sin to the mind. . . . So, *Messer Giorgio, mio caro*, please thank the Duke on my behalf for his magnificent offer of which you write, and beg his Excellency that with his grace and favour I may continue here long enough that in time I can at least leave with honour and with my good name untarnished. Your *Michelagnolo in Roma*.'

A letter to Vasari two years later shows that the master's anxieties are still troubling him:

Messer Giorgio, amico caro, I call upon God to witness how, against my will, and under the greatest compulsion, I was set by the Pope ten years ago to build St Peter's in Rome. Had this work continued now as in the past I should today be so far advanced that I could wish to go my way. But for lack of money there has been much delay, now that we have come to a very troublesome and difficult point. Were I to abandon it now, it would be with great dishonour and I should lose my whole reward for the work which I have endured, with God's help and mercy, for ten years.

I am writing you this letter in reply to yours, and because I have received a letter from the Duke which has given me great surprise because his Excellency has deigned to write, and with so much kind/ ness. Therefore I thank God and his Excellency as much as I am able. I am losing the thread, because I have lost my memory and power of thought and writing is a great trouble to me since it is not my art. The conclusion is that I cannot go. My leaving would certainly satisfy that gang of thieves and would wreck my work, perhaps even stop it for ever. Another reason is that I have various obligations and a house and other things, worth some thousand *scudi*; if I were to leave without permission, I cannot tell what would become of them. A third reason is that I am much troubled in my body by gravel – a stone in the side which I have had for many years. And *Maestro* Eraldo [Realdo Colombo, his doctor] can testify to this, for I have preserved my life by his help.

Well then, to travel there [to Florence] in order to return here afterwards I have no heart for, and to come there for good would require a good deal of time for winding up my affairs in such a way that I should have nothing more to think of.

Seven more years were to elapse before the city of Florence, Vasari, and the *Accademia del Disegno* could receive Tuscany's greatest son – and then it was to pay the last respect to his remains and honour his memory.

Of the honour done to him by Vasari, in including him as the only living artist in the 1550 edition of the *Lives*, the author himself remarks: 'And it should not be wondered at that I have described the life of Michelangelo while he is still alive. Though I had not thought that he would soon die, it seemed right to do him this humble service, so that when, like all other men, he must depart from his body, he will not face the death of his truly immortal works. Their fame will live on for as long as the world exists, through the reports of men and the pens of writers, in despite of envy and in contempt of death.'

Vasari's *Lives* as planned was to have included only Italian artists, but various distinguished foreign artists had lived in Italy and in many respects influenced its art; some of their works he knew at first hand and some through prints. The artists concerned were a number of 'Flemish' painters, among whom he includes Dutch and German. He speaks with respect (among others) of Hubert and Jan van Eyck, referring to the latter as the inventor of the art of painting in oils, and of Rogier van der Weyden, Petrus Christus, Hugo van der Goes, Albrecht Dürer, Pieter Breughel, Lucas van Leyden, and Quentin Massys.

Vasari's information about the 'Flemish' artists derives in large part from correspondence with the painter and architect Lambert Lombard of Liège and Dominicus Lampsonius, a scholar of Bruges. The latter had been secretary to the English cardinal, Reginald Pole (whom Vasari had portrayed in the *Cancelleria*), while he was serving as papal legate in Belgium and England. Having read the *Lives* in the first edition, he had immediately sent the author an enthusiastic letter of thanks. Vasari had taken the opportunity in his reply, to ask for information about Flemish artists, and Lampsonius soon sent him what he could find out about various painters, among them Martin Schongauer, and especially Dürer. The correspondence with this interested and amiable man, who had learnt Italian in order to study the art of Italy in its own language, lasted for three or four years.

CHAPTER V

Vasari's Sources and Material

HOW DID an art writer of Vasari's stature come to arise four hundred years ago? There was no school or chair for that kind of literary activity in those days; no developed tradition or anything in the way of professional journals; no reviewers to guide the interested student as there are today. Clearly, in a man called upon to discharge the task which fell to Vasari there had to be a lucky conjuncture of qualifications over and above technical and artistic training.

The accounts agree that already in his childhood at home in Arezzo, and later in Florence, Vasari acquired the contemporary culture to an exceptional degree. When presented to Cardinal Passerini at the age of thirteen, he could recite long passages from the *Aeneid* by heart in Latin, an accomplishment which lay well above the general level of school knowledge. As a young man he had read *Il divinissimo Dante, Il legiadro Petrarca*, and *L'amoroso Boccaccio*, and he was familiar with Ariosto and many other popular writers of his day. He read Latin easily, and must have found fascinating reading in the books of Vitruvius on architecture, which were a Bible to the profession. He was familiar with Greek and Roman archaeology and had a first-hand knowledge of many relics of classical antiquity. He was not well up in Greek, but he knew how to make the best use of his learned friends.

Below I shall suggest some of the chief sources that were available to Vasari. They differ both as to extent and character between the two editions of the *Lives*. As I have said, the material was much expanded and corrected for the 1568 edition, on which the work of later scholars has been almost entirely based. For the purpose of simplification, I propose to deal with this material together.

When embarking upon his biographies Vasari had, in the first place, to seek information about the artists who paved the way in the thirteenth and fourteenth centuries. He found names like Cimabue, Giotto, and Simone Martini extolled in imaginative literature by Dante and Petrarch, and he found further stories about artists in the tales of Boccaccio and Sachetti. In addition he found basic material in the 'professional' litera‑ ture. Ideas touching the rebirth of humanism and art lay in the air in the Florence of the fourteenth century. The names of important artists reached the general public not only through the work of poets but also through their own splendid decorations of churches and palaces. Historical authors were beginning to rank them with the celebrated sons of Tuscany. At this time the Florentine Giovanni Villani embarked on a chronicle of his city in twelve volumes, an undertaking continued by his brother Matteo and the latter's son Filippo.

Villani, a learned and travelled man, was the first historian to lift artists out of their traditional anonymity to a place of honour in the new culture. He must be given the credit for having recognized the 'primitive' painters of Florence and Siena as renewers of Graeco‑Roman painting. The first pioneer, he says, was Cimabue, who knew how to imitate nature; Giotto took the path opened up for him, and was not only the equal of the classical masters but their superior. He praises Giotto's character, which he finds reflected in his moral gifts, for he aspired to fame rather than to gain. He sees admirable qualities in this painter's successors, and especially in Giottino. 'He is the finest of them all, the grace of his painting being not only wonderful but incredible.' Villani here perceives a 'school' and the first germs of a new development. He is frequently quoted in detail by Vasari.

Besides comments and lists of names in *Il Libro Vecchio* belonging to the Florentine guild of painters, Vasari found material about the 'primitives' in a book by the painter Cennino di Drea Cennini (born 1372), who was a member of the school of Giotto. In this book, *Libro dell' Arte*, Cennino gives a general account of the procedures and technical experience of the time of Giotto, and he was aware that this master reshaped art 'from Greek to Latin', modernizing it and mastering it more fully than anyone had done before. A mere imitation of others, Cennino says, handicaps the formation of an individual style. 'Fundamental in art', he goes on, 'are design and colouring – design not only with your pen, but also with what you have in your head. . . . The good painter should work in his teacher's studio for seven years, and train himself practically in every way for a further seven . . . both on weekdays and on holidays; . . . he should always think of art as a love-offering to the divine.'

In the following century, the ideas of these writers were taken up by the unknown author of *The Life of Brunelleschi*; and later in the fifteenth century a Florentine priest, Francesco Albertini, published a book about his city's monuments, churches, palaces, relics, treasures and works of art.

About 1450 we meet one of the first artists to write on art, the sculptor and bronze-founder Lorenzo Ghiberti, who is best known for his doors to the baptistry of Florence Cathedral. He is no man of letters, nor does he aim at biographical or historical account as such; he wishes to preserve for posterity the memory of the artists who created those works which seem to him to be the best, and it is remarkable that he does not report the judgments of others but confines himself to the impact which the works have made on his own mind. In his *Commentari*, he especially supplements Villani by extending the circle of interest from his own Tuscany to Rome and also Siena. Among the artists of the latter city, he considers Ambrogio Lorenzetti to be the first painter of stature, thus contradicting the view of leading connoisseurs in Siena who awarded pride of place to Simone Martini. Ghiberti here allows us to guess at a Sienese tradition different from the Florentine. In his thoughts on the nature of art, he insists that painting consists not only in action and material but equally in the spirit of the work. In the *Lives*, Vasari employs a good deal of Ghiberti's material and devotes considerable space to his comments. It is therefore surprising that his reference to Ghiberti is as scornful as it is.

At about the same time, there appeared a voluminous work – of twenty-five books – from the hand of the architect and sculptor An

tonio Averlino, usually known as Filarete. Filarete's treatise on architecture is of prime interest; in it he especially deals with the measurements
and proportions of buildings, his philosophy and wide-ranging ideas
leading him to suggest to the Duke of Milan the construction of an ideal
town – in short, the introduction of town-planning! Vasari makes use of
Filarete's matter when describing various artists, but quotes him rather
superficially and scoffs at his fantastic plans.

Another work of great importance, providing a basis for Renaissance
theory, had also appeared in the fifteenth century. Its author was Leon
Battista Alberti, an artist who seems to have been equally eminent as
architect, mathematician, humanist and philosopher. In one of the first
volumes of his work, *Il Trattato della Pittura*, he formulates the rules of
painting more clearly than ever before. Postulating a product of the
artist's mind, the *idea*, to be realized by the work of his hand, he affirms
that it must no longer be regarded as outside the bounds of nature, but
must be divested of its transcendental character and considered as mathe-
matical knowledge about man. Certain principles will emerge from
the desire for plastic form: outlines of figures must be imperceptible,
consisting of a margin of surface and not a gulf; it is essential to draw a
nude before painting the clothes on it, to render bones and muscles
before putting flesh on them.

Vasari was very familiar with the work of Alberti, which has been
called by a later age the Magna Carta of the Renaissance; yet he makes
strikingly little use of it, and seems insufficiently appreciative.

Other contributions to the formulation and elaboration of Vasari's
theoretical ballast were the examples of Paolo Uccello and Piero della
Francesca, both of whom had devoted much time and thought to
speculations on the laws of linear perspective.

That other great genius of the fifteenth century, Leonardo da Vinci,
was bound to attract Vasari's interest. Leonardo, who had spent in-
finitely more time in pondering and experimenting on the nature of
things and on the potentialities of technique than he had on his painting,
left a mass of notes about painting: material which was to a large extent
available to Vasari. Leonardo's manuscripts, including the *Treatise on*

Painting, went mostly to his heir, the painter Francesco Melzi, whom Vasari was able to visit and talk with. The notes, edited later, were published in 1651. Although Vasari was familiar with Leonardo's ideas about the posing and grouping of figures, his *Contrapposto*, as well as his theories on the use of light, his *Chiaroscuro* and *Sfumato*, they do not seem to have made more than an academic impression on him. Vasari was incapable of following him in practice, but he must have been at one with Leonardo where the latter says that 'painting is not only science, it is divine, because it transforms the painter's spirit into something equal to the spirit of God.'

In 1553 Ascanio Condivi, who was a pupil and friend of Michelangelo, published a biography which was largely Michelangelo's autobiography, and which to a certain extent may be read as a reply to the first edition of Vasari's *Lives*. Condivi denied, for example, that Michelangelo had been apprenticed to Ghirlandaio, a fact which Michelangelo apparently wished to be forgotten. Vasari's greatly expanded biography of Michelangelo in the second edition of the *Lives* was his answer to Condivi; in it he printed the actual articles of apprenticeship.

Besides material in the chroniclers, Vasari found information about many artists in the attribution and dating of works in monastic and church records, as well as in legal documents, contracts, signatures, and inscriptions on buildings and other works of art.

But his most graphic and fascinating material from the point of view of the modern reader, because it illustrates the life and manners of the time, is that which derives from oral sources, including a great many conversations with the descendants of artists then dead, as well as with friends and relatives of some who were still alive. Long before he ever thought of writing his book, his insatiable curiosity had procured him reports and data from his friends and clients. The most prevalent stories were about 'popular' artists like Brunelleschi, Donatello, Ghiberti and Castagno, and, nearer to his own time, Leonardo, Raphael and Michelangelo. Vasari employs this personal information less for any systematization than for human characterization, whether to laud or disparage.

On his travels, when he would avidly study the pictures of predecessors, he used to seek out monks and churchmen, who furnished him
with traditional information about the origins of works of art, and provided vivid impressions of famous artists – their appearance, dress,
habits, and methods of working – interwoven with chronicles and
legends.

It is probable, and indeed in many cases it is a fact, that much in these
stories, which had travelled from monastery to monastery, transmitted
often by old people, was garbled, being frequently no more than unreliable gossip and old wives' tales. Many later editors have pounced
on unreliable and untrue stories in Vasari's work, but with Adolfo
Venturi we may take a lenient view of all this. 'Imagine', he says, 'how
much would have been lost but for Vasari; . . . the greatest and most
prolific of his sources was the constant rediscovery and returning to works
which were centuries old, in order to see and see once more (*vedere e rive-
dere*).' 'Without Vasari and his incomparably important work,' says
Jacob Burckhardt, 'there would be no art history in the North, or in
Europe at all.'

Vasari's source material also included a quantity of letters. He was
able to trace many which had been exchanged, generations earlier,
between artists, or between artists and scholars and other influential
people. But it was especially in his own day that letter-writing played a
prominent part in cultural life.

Vasari was always a diligent correspondent; to communicate his desires, thoughts, plans and suggestions by letter came naturally and easily
to him, though he would occasionally say that he preferred to express
himself, and did so best, with the brush. It had been known since his
death that many letters had been preserved; some were in the collection
of his nephew, Messer Marcantonio Vasari, and some were in official
archives in the Vatican, elsewhere in Rome, at Pisa, Arezzo, Venice
and Florence, but the majority of them had been missing for centuries.
A certain number, deriving chiefly from the State Archives at Florence,
the Archivio Riccardiano, eventually came to light. Bottari used some
of these in his Rome edition of the *Lives* and others were made available

46 *Iacopo Pontormo: The Resurrection. One of his Certosa frescoes (see p. 37).*

(see p. 37)

47 *Andrea del Sarto: Birth of the Virgin Mary.*

48 Raphael: The Prophet Isaiah (see p. 114).

to Milanesi, who used them in his edition of 1878 and thereafter. There were gaps in his material, however, since many of the replies, in particular, were missing.

In 1908 Giovanni Poggi, Italian art historian and director of the Bargello in Florence, discovered while engaged in other research that the bulk of the original collection of Vasari papers was deposited in private archives in Florence, owned by Count Rasponi-Spinelli. The last of the Vasari, the priest Francesco Maria Vasari, had given the letters to his executor, Senator Bonsignore Spinelli, intending that they should afterwards go to the Fraternità dei Laici at Arezzo. In 1910 the matter came to the knowledge of Karl Frey, a German Vasari scholar, and by means of strong diplomatic aid and a generous grant from the German Government, he acquired the sole right to edit and publish the 'Rasponi papers' in German. With the addition of some letters discovered later in Britain and America, the collection, *Il Carteggio di Giorgio Vasari*, totalled 1054 items, of which 400 are by Vasari, largely in his own hand, the rest having been written by scribes. Frey began to edit the material, drafting commentaries and getting most of it ready for the press. He died before the work could be completed, but his son and associate, Hermann-Walther Frey, did so and published it in three volumes in 1923, 1930 and 1940. The texts are printed in Italian with the original orthography, the commentaries being in German.

The news of the discovered treasure and the German scoop aroused bitterness among Italian art historians, who thought that the deal had been transacted in an underhand manner. Pio Pecchiai writes in his edition of the *Lives*: ' . . . it is deplorable that a foreigner should do this, that we should be studying a basic work of our own culture in a foreign language . . . . with all the conceited Teutonic industry, going to the lengths of sheer pedantry.' After the death of Karl Frey, moreover, it was feared that it would be a long time before the publication of the papers could be completed; and Rasponi-Spinelli having transferred them to Arezzo where they had been deposited in the Casa Vasari, the curator of the collection, Professor Alessandro del Vita, began to publish annotated material from the Carteggio. This took place in a journal founded and edited by him, *Il Vasari*, which acquainted the Italian public with Vasari's literary remains over a long period of years from 1927. This material was collected and published by the Reale Istituto d'Archeologia e Storia dell'Arte, Rome and Arezzo, in 1938–41.

The publication of the Vasari papers has greatly added to the picture of the man and his work, in that personal contemporary statements, characteristic of both sender and recipient, reflect moods, sentiments of friendship, displeasure, sincerity, dissimulation, jest, sarcasm – all those features which illuminate the writer's personality.

Among these letters are many of mainly businesslike character, concerning projects, plans, and technical matters. Many – to and from Vasari – discuss fees, concessions and favours, or express congratulation or condolence. The most arresting are those which come from the heart, requesting and giving advice, conveying information and suggestions, ideas and inventions; those that are marked by pleasure at artistic productions, journeys and financial successes; and those which describe friends and enemies, or reflect the writer's own personal ambition and vanities.

We find all these things in Vasari's letters. The correspondents include popes, writing – or causing to be written – in Latin, and cardinals who sign themselves 'dearest friend and brother'. Letters to and from Michelangelo and others have already been quoted above. A great many of the letters have to do with Duke Cosimo, with his intense interest in art, his zeal as a collector, and his delight in building. He desired personally to discuss and correspond with his court artist about every detail. The correspondence with him begins in 1550, with Vasari's humble petition for permanent employment by him, and the same year sees the beginning of the discussion, which lasts until 1564, about the restoration and decoration of the Palazzo Vecchio. Vasari's letters are matter-of-fact, clear, and concise in statement and suggestion, with spaces left open at appropriate points for the Duke's comments, these being often very brief, as '*Va bene*' or '*Sta bene*'. For several years it was mostly a question of the construction of the Uffizi and the buildings of the Knights of Santo Stefano at Pisa.

Occasionally, letters from Vasari contain a *supplica* for fees over and above the fixed salary, as in 1568, 'concerning the scenes in the great hall of the palace:

For each of the IIII large scenes in fresco	300 ducats
For each of the II smaller scenes	200 ducats
For each of the IIII scenes in oils	100 ducats
Total	2,000 ducats

Further, on the ground floor, 12 scenes at 100 ducats each, total 1200'.

Salaries for assistants were included in these sums, which were immediately granted.

Gradually, the Duke's letters take on a note of friendly intimacy, and Vasari is entrusted with numerous private commissions. Thus the Duke asks him to assist in finding and acquiring objects of art and anti- quities. In 1558, when Cosimo is establishing a gallery of famous men, he instructs Vasari to attend to the collection or production of copies, especially from Giovio's collection of over two hundred and fifty portraits, and to ensure that no one else had any opportunity to copy. For his part, whenever he has ferreted out anything extra-special, Vasari always remembers to notify the Duke. Thus when he has dis- covered in Rome that a classical sculpture, afterwards famous, is for sale, the Duke writes to him: 'I tell you that We are resolved to have "The Peasant Sharpening a Knife", and since you say that the owner of it is ready to sell it for 800 *scudi*, if you cannot get it for less – snap it up at all costs! And the ambassador and you should seek a licence from His Holiness to remove it from Rome and bring it here, and we wish it to come by land and not by sea.' The work in question was the re- nowned 'Knife-sharpener', found during digging in the Monte Pincio, which can now be seen in the Tribuna of the Uffizi.

A letter in which Vasari opens his full and devoted heart to the Duke – and at the same time throws an interesting light on himself – was written in 1564. For page after page he dwells on the wonderful fortune which has come to him in the founding of his own chapel at Arezzo. He goes into every detail, of stone, marble, bronze, wood, stucco, oil and gold, in his work. 'Nor have I there', he writes,

plate 12
p. 46

> omitted to honour the memory of Lazzaro Vasari, a celebrated painter in his day, and Giorgio, his son, my grandfather, who was an architect; there are also portraits of my father and mother. [Next to them Vasari portrayed his wife and himself in the guise of S. Lazzaro and S. Maddalena.] Their bones have been placed to-gether in a tomb below the altar, in the middle of the chancel. Here I believe these tired bones will rest as long as God pleases, so that their spirits will be worthy of His glory. Next after God and His saints, I can thank you, my most gracious lord, for the honour which has befallen me by the consecration of this work and for such great gifts – and bless your illustrious Highness who, with the appro-bation of His saints, has enabled me by means of money and assist-ance in all ways to achieve such a work under such favourable con-ditions. It has been the cause of the recreation and resurrection of this church – so venerated and so beloved – in the heart of this city, and has given encouragement to the canons, enabling them to maintain it and celebrate masses there better than before.
>
> And if God grant me life, I hope also – with the generosity which your Excellency will extend to my works – to make this offering to Him: I hereby declare that the great God who made me worthy of your service has willed that I should partake of your greatness and leave to my country and my fellow-citizens so honourable a remem-brance, shedding lustre on this poor house of mine . . . and this town whose population will be admired and contented by the donation – so unexpectedly and so soon – of a work so large and so serviceable that it will be held in honour and remembrance for generations to come of your Excellency and
>
> your Giorgio.

Once during the work on the Uffizi when Vasari had trouble both with the supervisory committee and with colleagues and workmen, who threatened to complain of him to the Duke, the latter, who had got wind of the affair, possibly through Vasari himself, writes: 'Remember that Florentines always stick together in battle and that they regard you as an Aretine and not a Florentine; do not get involved in all their quarrelling, and remember that you can never get two Florentines to agree.'

In Cosimo's last letter, written in 1573, the year in which both died, he expresses his pleasure that Giorgio has succeeded so well in Rome, and hopes to see him back in Florence to work on the dome of the cathedral.

Most of the letters are to and from his lifelong friend Don Vincenzo Borghini, Dominican prior, and later superior of the Foundling Hospital, *Ospedale degli Innocenti*, in Florence. He was of the same age as Giorgio, reserved by nature, frail in health – to all appearances a neurasthenic and a sufferer from gastric ulcers, but intelligent, lucid, well-informed, indeed learned, and always tactful and friendly – a tireless helper and adviser in everything, from ideas for monumental pictures to mediating in marital affairs and drawing up wills. He was an invaluable support for Vasari during the preparation of the *Lives*; not on the artistic side, for there Vasari was his superior, but in matters of editorial technique, stylistic presentation, and the procuring of literary sources. Borghini was convinced of the book's value as a specialized history, and its importance to the nation's intellectual development. Deeply interested in the visual arts, he collected prints and was personally acquainted with a great many artists. With unquestionable business talent, he arranged commissions and agreements between artists and clients, acting in many cases as Duke Cosimo's adviser and agent. When the Academy was founded, the Duke made him his *luogotenente*, or vice-president.

plate 19
p. 48

Borghini regretted his misfortune in never meeting Michelangelo face to face, and he gives expression to his thoughts on this in a letter to Vasari: '. . . I envy you the friendship and confidence of the greatest genius our generation has known, and when I think of how Boccaccio, speaking of Giotto, called him one of the greatest luminaries in the aureole of Florence, I believe I do not exaggerate when I say that he could in no way compare with Michelangelo. I think that Boccaccio would have been dumbfounded to know that the world would one day produce the equal, not to say superior, of him [Giotto]; that was why he expressed himself so strongly and awarded him this honourable name, which in truth was first deserved by Messer Michelangelo, whom I envy you with all my heart; not in the sense that you should not be allowed to enjoy him as you do, but that I might have a share in doing so. For I assure you that I should die content, had I experienced such a favour as that of enjoying the friendship of so great a man. Whether the future will look upon his like I cannot say, but certainly the past never did.'

Another long-standing friend met with in the letters is Cosimo Bartoli; trained for the priesthood, he was chiefly engaged in writing and translating, and was for many years the Duke's agent in Venice. He was an untiring letter-writer, who sent a vast amount of information about the art of Venice, and about the life and work of its artists. Moreover, he was at home in commercial and political matters, and was admirably informed about the private lives of every important person. He is very flattering to Vasari, and asks him without embarrassing modesty for assistance in obtaining favours and for pictures by him.

One of those whom Vasari had known longest in Florence was Guglielmo Sangaletti, who, on leaving for Rome, became private secretary to Pope Pius v. In that influential position he formed a natural link between the Curia and Vasari, and it may be accounted to his credit that Vasari in his later years received large commissions from the Pope, and also that the Pope made him a knight of the Golden Spur and St Peter, carrying an endowment of 1200 *scudi*, and awarded him the magnificent Chain of Favour in gold which adorns Vasari's breast in the self-portrait now in the Uffizi. (Vasari in his meticulous accounts values the chain at 80 gold *scudi*.)

plate 20
p. 48
Alongside his busy activities as an author and letter-writer, that other native of Arezzo, Pietro Aretino, found time for a lively correspondence with Giorgio, the friend of his youth. His friendship seems actually to have been sincere, though it did not stop him from bartering recommendations, instructive letters, and even indulgences in return for pictures

and other objects of art. Altogether, it is evident from many letters – and this is true of many others besides Vasari and Aretino – that one good turn deserves another: a sentiment which finds rather more candid expression than is the custom now. The correspondence lasted for at least fifteen years, from 1534 to about 1550.

The tone and temper of Vasari's letters are characterized for the most part by his sober outlook and cool head, but there are exceptions. In writing to the Duke he goes to great lengths of servility, and his letters to Michelangelo, for whom he had boundless admiration, radiate genuine respect and warm devotion. It is therefore remarkable that in addressing Aretino he seems humble and at times downright obsequious. It is true that Aretino was surrounded by an air of awe, but the fact remains that he came from 'back home'. Vasari sometimes styles him *Divinissimo*, a form of address which he generally reserves for Michel-angelo.

In reply to a letter from Aretino, written about 1534, he begins: 'As Phoebus displays himself in his most resplendent rays after the arrival of Aurora, shining down upon the mountains and the rest of our grand old mother [Earth] in his brightest lustre and bringing nourishment to her who bestows life upon all her creatures, so have you enlightened my spirit, so has the power in the sound of your voice, as set down by you in such happy characters, inspired me to return thanks to God that you should have laid the snowy-white sheets before your candles and with your right hand have seized the pen, vouchsafing to write to one who merits neither to hear from you nor to know of matters which are yours. . . .'

Either Vasari really intended to flatter his mighty correspondent, or by the use of such flowery language he was indulging – as seems more likely – in heavy sarcasm at his friend's expense.

From another reply it appears that Aretino has pleased Giorgio by calling him 'Son', and also by moralizing to him, urging him to keep to the path of virtue and indicating the prospect of his shedding lustre on Arezzo, their common birthplace. In return for all this he asks for a picture from Giorgio's hand.

Vasari then writes:

Your reasonable desire that in return for the protection accorded to me in regarding me as your son you should receive a work from my hand, leads me to say that I shall endeavour to send you by the next mail one of the cartoons at which I have been working for the corner room of the Palazzo Medici. . . . It shows him [Caesar] in Egypt, when, in the naval battle between him and Ptolemy, he envisages the risk of defeat and plunges into the waves, holding his book on the Gallic wars in one hand and swimming with the other until he arrives in safety at the opposite shore. . . .

If the picture pleases you I shall be gratified, since you express the desire that there should arise in your native town of Arezzo and in your own time a painter capable of making figures to speak with his hands; and since you appear to believe that God has granted your desire, you ask me to set aside youth's desire for pleasures, lest the intellect go astray and become sterile, with the result that I should be unable to create the fruits which bring immortality. . . .

Let these words suffice, Messer Pietro, *mio caro*, for one whom the spirit has inspired to fame, indeed great fame, among the most nobly gifted. Do not doubt but that I shall exert myself, Heaven granting me the strength, that you shall have the good fortune to see Arezzo, the city which has blossomed in arms and in literature but where I cannot find that there has previously arisen a painter out of the ordinary, succeed in melting the ice in me and enable me to finish the studies which I have begun. . . . Keep in good health and do not forget me who desire one day to see you again; and pay my respects to Sansovino and Titian. And when you have received the cartoon which I am sending you, please let me know their opinon as well as your own.

Another member of Vasari's circle of close friends was Don Miniato Pitti, a man of noble family and of wide general culture, who after a theological training had become abbot of the monastery of San Benedetto at Pistoia, and afterwards of San Bernardo at Arezzo, but who

49 *Leonardo: Head of St Anne (detail of 'St Anne, the Virgin and Child'). 'He outstrips all other men, manifesting his genius as a gift of God rather than a human acquirement.'*

50 *Michelangelo: The Delphic Sibyl. Detail from the ceiling of the Sistine Chapel.*

51 Correggio: The Madonna and Child with St Jerome (detail). 'No one handled colour better than he did.'

52 Giovanni Bellini: The Dead Christ with His Mother and St John.

53 *Giorgione: The Three Philosophers (see p. 111).*

54 *Titian: Venus with a Dog. 'The greatest master of our day.'*

55 *Sebastiano del Piombo:*
Andrea Doria.

56 *Andrea del Sarto: Lucrezia del Fede. Lucrezia was*
the artist's wife, and, according to Vasari, left him to
die alone when he contracted the plague. But Vasari's
evidence seems biased and unreliable (see p. 154).

preferred the occupation of writing literary papers on mathematics, mechanics and astronomy, and was well informed on aesthetic matters. Very devoted to Giorgio, he was for many years his unselfish helper, convinced as he was of the merit of his friend's art. He arranged many a good commission for Giorgio from members of the aristocracy and monastic colleagues, and he was a tireless collector of material for the *Lives* besides being a great help, as a fine stylist, in shaping and editing the material. Pitti was a lively letter-writer: gay, witty, and free from malice.

In a letter from Rome dated 1563 he writes to Vasari: '. . . The other morning Michelangelo Buonarroti, accompanied by two young grooms, came to mass in our church. He said that he knew me, as he had been a friend of my father's, and we spoke for perhaps half an hour. I told him of the great respect and devotion which you entertain for him, and of the building of the Uffizi and the Salon [the great hall of the Palazzo Vecchio], and the many pictures of great figures which you have made there. He was loud in your praises, and said that you had fallen in with a prince who desires to create great and laudable things and that you should comply with his wishes.

'I told him about the work which you are doing to recreate the lives of the painters, and about the portraits, those excellent woodcuts; he was much pleased by this, and said that single-handed you did the work of more than a thousand men.'

plate 18
p. 48

One of the most remarkable personalities of his time, Paolo Giovio, is also represented among Vasari's correspondents. Born in 1485, and so Vasari's senior by twenty-six years, he had been trained like most scholars at that time as a theologian, and, as Bishop of Nocera, was secretary to Cardinal Alessandro Farnese. He had also had a medical training, and was for a period physician to Pope Clement. Under the name of Paulus Iovius, however, he was best known as the author of a history of Italy and Europe, written in Latin.

As a person Giovio was impulsive, sarcastic, sometimes unfeeling, and frequently coarse. Possibly his manner was determined by his physical infirmity; often he was obliged to spend weeks and even months in bed with the gout, and in addition to the familiar symptoms of podagra he had the corresponding ones in the right hand known as chiragra. It may be added that he was a great gourmet. Letters to Vasari on the occasion of the latter's approaching marriage, showing specimens of his style, have been quoted above; but he also wrote many useful and informative epistles, mostly about the 'Book'. Besides being its original inspirer, he was one of the chosen censors. The first to receive the recently completed manuscript in 1547, he wrote to Vasari: '*Eccel-lentissimo Messer Giorgio mio*. I swallowed your book – *subito, subito* – immediately on receiving it, and remain altogether astonished at that which seemed impossible: that you, who can do so much with the brush, should so distinguish yourself by the pen. . . . And die and perish those who envy you for it! You are my better: you who will become immortal!'

CHAPTER VI

The Style and the Man

VASARI'S STYLE brought a renewal in the literature of the period. Writing to him at the start of the work, his friend Borghini had urged him: 'Do not write too elaborately or too formally, but let your style resemble natural everyday speech.' Following this advice, Vasari wrote neither in Latin nor in the stilted contemporary Italian but in an idiom which, in the opinion of the experts, is a fresh and flowing *lingua toscana*, as distinct from that of his contemporary and fellow-artist, Benvenuto Cellini, who rattles away, in his autobiography, in an unadulterated *lingua volgare*.

In the *Lives* Vasari introduced a number of technical expressions which have become standard terms in art literature. Towards the end of the work he writes:

> But to bring a long story to a close: I have written as a painter, and in the order I thought best; and as for the language (whether it be called Florentine or Tuscan), in the manner that seemed most natural and easy, leaving ornate and lengthy periods, variations of voice, and other ornaments of style, as well as scholarly writing, to those who are, like me, better hands with the brush than with the pen, and have better heads for design than for writing. If at various points in the work I have deliberately employed terms which are special to our art, rather than the more splendid expressions of our language, I have done so to avoid misunderstanding and in order to be understood by you artists for whom I principally undertook this work.

'The style is altogether Vasari's,' Adolfo Venturi says; 'an undoubted biographer, he has remained unexcelled as an historian *sui generis*.'

As the reader will have seen from the foregoing examples, Vasari is fond of opening his chapters with philosophical observations on the gifts of Heaven and Nature and man's administration of them, always emphasizing the importance of universal human qualities to an artist's development, alongside the value which lies in tradition and broadly based training. What Vasari's account of art may lack, for good reasons, in the systematics of art history is amply made up for by his tireless, efficient, and often repeated personal inspection. He has 'seen everything', he says.

His narration, though it can be rather dry and detailed in the enumeration of works by individual artists, is absorbing and frequently spiced with picturesque anecdotes and stories, exciting and dramatic, if not always authentic. In the first edition of the *Lives* especially he was not over-scrupulous with regard to authenticity, but for him as for any other historian that depended on the reliability of the sources. A curious touch is the one mentioned by W. Schorn: the work had to be so complete that the biography of an important artist had to end with his epitaph. If there was none, Vasari either wrote one himself or got someone else to write one. (Some of these false epitaphs were omitted from the second edition.) Wishing to place his own person in the most favourable light, he takes liberties with the facts. When taken, as a model of industry, to Florence, he was not, as he states, eleven, but thirteen years of age; when he obtained regular employment with the Duke at Florence he was not, as he writes, eighteen, but twenty-six.

There is a chapter in the *Lives* about a certain Lazzaro Vasari of Arezzo, Giorgio's great-grandfather. 'Lazzaro', says our author, 'was in his day a painter famous in all Tuscany . . . a close friend of Piero della Francesca, with whom he associated daily and whom he much resembled in style.' As time went on scholars began to think it strange that no other writer had mentioned the painter Lazzaro, and that none of his works had been preserved. After extensive research in the archives, Milanesi asserts that Lazzaro was not a painter but a saddler, and moreover that he died long before Piero della Francesca was painting in Arezzo.

In judging his fellow-artists, and especially his contemporaries, Vasari's professional heart is filled with enthusiasm for those who attract him, but he coldly dismisses those whom he does not like. He is not seldom malicious, though he is at pains to keep his artistic appraisal distinct from the personal. It is characteristic of him that he is far more ready to admit artistic merits in his colleagues than literary ones, and in the latter respect one senses indeed a touch of real envy.

Writing of Lorenzo Ghiberti as an author, Vasari passes the following judgment: 'The same Lorenzo wrote a work . . . from which one can derive little benefit, . . . discussing great artists too briefly, . . . writing chiefly in order to speak of himself and detail his own works . . ., using the first person, as: "*I* said, *I* did. . . ."' This is quite certainly a distorted and unfair picture of the engaging Ghiberti, whose precise merit is that he relies chiefly on what he has personally seen and experienced of works of art.

Vasari's view of the literary work of Filarete is that 'although there is some good in these books, yet they are mostly ridiculous and vain. If with all the pains he took he had at least thought of the artists of his time and their works, it would have been possible to praise him for something. About them there is little information, and that little scattered, disconnected and ill-arranged, so that, as one might say, he took pains to belittle . . . aiming to appear well-informed himself in undertaking what he did not understand.'

At various points in the *Lives* Vasari inserts moral reproofs, and rules of living and working, which he himself forgets to adhere to. He is a severe judge of human vacillation. This is his assessment of Francesco Salviati, the friend of his youth: 'Francesco was an excellent painter. Friendly, though melancholy, to begin with, he in time became envious, looking down on more ordinary artists, showing himself capricious, difficult and avaricious, and consequently making himself many enemies who spoke disparagingly of him, though Vasari on all occasions tried to take his part.'

The painting of Sebastiano del Piombo and Vasari's opinion of it have already been referred to. Sebastiano's success in obtaining a minor but permanent appointment was clearly a thorn in the flesh for Vasari, but we will allow him to tell the story himself:

> Sebastiano was in great favour with Pope Clement VII; and at the death of the holder of the papal seal this office was awarded to Sebastiano, who had thus, according to protocol, to don the cowl of a friar. . . . It at once became apparent that he had changed his behaviour; realizing that he was now able to achieve his desires without lifting a brush, he took his ease, rewarding himself for earlier sleepless nights and days of toil by his income and prosperity . . . yet whenever he had work to do, doing it with as much passion as if it were a matter of life and death. . . . Thus may one see how much confusion arises between our words and our poor human judgments, which frequently, and indeed invariably, desire the opposite of what is beneficial; so that when men think they are crossing themselves they poke their fingers in their eyes, as we say in a Tuscan proverb. In this case the generous liberality shown by Clement to an admirable artist from Venice converted by rich rewards an industrious painter into a negligent idler. . . . From that time on he was to be numbered among the 'lost'.

How far Vasari could go in rancour and bitterness is illustrated by one or two examples. Of his revered friend and mentor, Andrea del Sarto, he says: 'Andrea married rather suddenly and precipitately' – in short, without consulting his friends! Lucrezia del Fede, the young wife of a hatter, had set her cap at Andrea and in Vasari's opinion seduced the good-natured artist, obliging him to marry her after the early death of her husband. Time after time, however, she was unfaithful to him, causing him all the pangs of jealousy, in addition to domineering him and bleeding him for the benefit of her family and to the neglect of his own. She also domineered and bullied the artist's pupils – the sort of behaviour that pupils refuse to accept from the wife of a teacher. When Andrea fell ill with the plague during the siege of Florence, his wife, afraid of contracting the disease herself, left him to die alone, according to Vasari. Scholars are now of the opinion that Vasari's hostility to her

derives from these domestic conditions, since for a short period he was
one of the pupils who suffered under her domination in Andrea's house,
and they believe the account to be based on an extremely loose, not to
say untrue, foundation. A portrait of Lucrezia, splendidly painted by
Andrea, is now in the Prado in Madrid, and represents her as a very
charming woman.

plate 56
p. 148

The roughest treatment of all, however, is reserved for Andrea del
Castagno:

the faithless Andrea, an important painter, yet one in whom envy
and hatred of other painters were far stronger. . . . Andrea painted in
Florence along with Domenico Veneziano, who had taught the
Tuscan painters to work in oils. Andrea displayed very great abilities, especially in design, but he was less successful in his colouring,
there being something hard and coarse about it. He was best in the
movements and expression of the men and women whom he painted.
Had nature endowed him with skill in colouring, as it bestowed
upon him vigour of composition and design, he would surely have
been accounted admirable.

Being as cunning a hypocrite as he was admirable as a painter, he
was gay when he wished, sharp-tongued as well as cool-headed and in
every action of his body as resolute as he was in his mind. He was
animated by the same spirit towards other artists as well as Domenico,
and it was his habit, whenever he saw a fault in the work of a colleague, to scratch it secretly with his nail in order to emphasize the
fault. Even in his youth, if anyone criticized one of his works he
would make it clear, by blows and insults, that he was both able
and ready to take his revenge. . . .

How blameworthy, in an otherwise excellent personality, is the
vice of envy, which should be found in no one. And how criminal
and dreadful it is when someone, under pretext of friendship, seeks to
deprive others not only of their reputation and honour, but of life
itself. For the baseness of such behaviour beggars the resources of
even the most eloquent tongue.

Thus, harbouring resentment and jealousy of his friendly colleague he resolved to make away with him. One day when Domenico was walking in the street, with his lute over his shoulder, Andrea, disguised and wearing a mask, waylaid him, crushed first his lute and then his head with a bar of lead, and, leaving him there to die, hurried home to the studio they shared, and feigned the greatest grief when they brought home Domenico's body. The villainy would never have been found out, but for the fact that Andrea confessed to it on his death-bed.

Exhaustive studies of original documents have disproved this gruesome story. While it is true that Andrea was of a hot-tempered and jealous disposition, which justified his poor reputation, it was in his work, rather than in his general conduct, that he was aggressive and belligerent. What is more, Domenico survived Andrea by several years!

Vasari's original manuscript of the *Lives* has failed to survive and was probably destroyed immediately after printing, as was the general practice. His syntax and orthography have been intensively studied in order to determine, by analysing the style, whether any of his literary friends were responsible for parts of the work. Such direct contributions have not been established, but certainly there are opinions and viewpoints which bear the mark of Borghini, and indeed he was authorized to make additions and corrections. It has been established that passages in the text were influenced by Aretino, Giovio, and others; while the very detailed indexes were the work of Don Miniato Pitti.

Vasari's style is marked by the rather lax attitude to prose-writing of those days. His syntax is by no means irreproachable. He will frequently leave a train of thought unfinished, inserting dependent clauses in the middle of a period which break the connection, and there are sentences that are left unfinished. Often there are additions which are organically unconnected with the rest of the text; and when making corrections he sometimes omits to delete the part that was wrong.

I shall try below to summarize and define Vasari's position as an aesthetic and art-historical writer. His judgment of an artist's pictures is nearly always determined by their immediate impact. He knew an immense number at first hand, and he was extremely responsive, quick, and acutely perceptive in the presence of works of art, though the study and description of them always takes place in the light of his own ortho-dox school and technique. In his studies of the history of art from classical times to his own day he was fascinated by its fluctuations, and felt the profound degradation, indeed destruction, of his country's art during the medieval migrations and, in their wake, four or five hundred years of war, rapine, fire and havoc. He detects – about the time leading to the year 1000 – certain progress and fresh activity in church, castle and urban architecture, followed by a further spread of mosaic and fresco art, chiefly dispensed by 'Greek' (*i.e.* Byzantine) artists. As a Tuscan he is fired by the spirit and atmosphere which in the Duecento, and especially Trecento, heralded a new era: he sees the art of painting born anew.

Inspired by the writings of Villani, Cennino, and other earlier authors, influenced by books of the Quattrocento on art and by the works of the great painters of that century, he becomes convinced that a mighty reaction is setting in against the decline of the Middle Ages.

The great currents running through the three hundred years of the *Lives* are most clearly defined in the introduction to the second and third parts of the work. As he sees it, these centuries fall into three great periods, forming part of a long evolution. Explaining why he takes this view, he says that he 'will speak of these matters generally, not only in regard to persons, but also respecting the characteristics which are peculiar to the periods'.

In the first period, which he dates from the middle of the thirteenth century down to the close of the fourteenth, he sees the three arts as yet far from perfection and deserving little praise. At the same time, he commends the period because he sees in it ways and means which are leading to the good things that are to follow.

In the second period, covering approximately the first two-thirds of the fifteenth century, Vasari sees the disappearance of the clumsiness, formlessness, and lack of skill characteristic of the earlier period, and a great improvement both in design and execution, with better draughts-manship, style and care. Yet he thinks that even in this period there is no artist who is in every respect perfect: in invention, design, colour, or subtle transitions of outline and shades of colour, with the light remaining visible only in the highlights. This praise he reserves for the third period, which extends from the close of the fifteenth century down to his own time, when 'I think it may definitely be said that art has gone as far it is possible to go in the imitation of nature, and has advanced to such heights that there is fear of a decline rather than hope of a further rise.'

Reflecting carefully on these matters, I am inclined to think that it was inherent in the peculiar and special nature of the arts that from an inferior beginning they should steadily improve and finally reach the peak of perfection, and I am confirmed in my belief by the obser-vation that the same has been true of other human skills, there being a kinship between all the free arts. This provides no little proof of the truth of my assertion.

In this chapter of the work Vasari goes more fully into his ideas. In the manner of Giotto and his pupils, later esteemed and imitated, the outlines which surrounded the figures in the Byzantine period, the wide-open eyes, the tip-toeing feet, the tapered hands, were rejected and the lack of shading and other gross effects were overcome, and instead an appealing grace was achieved in the rendering of heads, as well as a broadly toned colouring. Giotto in particular showed improved posing: for the first time he gave life to the facial features, came nearer to nature than anyone before him in the folds of his drapery, and soon discovered something about perspective and foreshortening. Furthermore, he made a beginning in the rendering of states of mind, making expressions of fear, hope, anger, and love fairly recognizable. In his manner of paint-ing, softness took the place of the former hard and angular manner.

Giotto fails, in Vasari's opinion, to express the beautiful carefree glance of the eye, the softness of the hair, the downiness of the beard, the muscles and sinews of the body and hands, or the realism of the nude, but he makes allowances for these deficiencies, since he knew no painter who did better.

The followers of Giotto are also given some credit, because they retained his style, line and colour, and even brought about some improvement, 'though not so much as to make it look as if they were striving for another and higher purpose'. He also believed he had demon- strated that though painting had emancipated itself from its crudities it was still far from perfect, and but for the fact that later it had developed further, not even this initial step would have been very fruitful. 'Nor would I wish', he says, 'to be thought of as so incompetent and so lacking in judgment as not to appreciate that the pictures of Giotto and others, when compared with those of later artists, are not of any great or even moderate value. This was perfectly clear to me, indeed, when I praised them; but one must take into consideration the general conditions of the time, as well as the small number of artists and the poor patronage and support which they enjoyed. In short, these works would appear to us not so much beautiful as remarkable; and it is a very great pleasure to see initiative and the first sparks of what is good beginning to light up in painting and sculpture.'

In the second period Vasari detects considerable progress: the com- position richer in figures that are more beautifully adorned; the design more assured and more in accordance with nature; the style more attractive; the colours more pleasant. All this he sees manifest in 'the admirable Masaccio, who did away altogether with the manner of Giotto . . . introducing and establishing the modern style which artists have followed ever since. Through him his successors thought more deeply and with greater understanding about art, and so were en- couraged to formulate rules of perspective and foreshortening, as well as fresh views about light and shade. They achieved a far greater resem- blance to real life in their compositions, a contributing factor being their experiments in the production of landscapes with trees, flowers, air, clouds and other natural phenomena. In short, the arts have at last completed their education and unfolded themselves in the finest bloom of their youth.'

Thanks to the inspiration gained from the masters of the preceding period, the artists of the third period succeeded in attaining to an even higher level, sharing in 'that supreme perfection which justifies the special praise and fame that is due to our modern art. . . . The style developed into the sublimest beauty from the habit of copying the most beautiful things and adding to them their special features, whether hands, heads, body, or legs, so forming a figure of the greatest possible number of individual parts. Called for this reason 'the beautiful', this style was employed for every figure in every work.

This third period has arrived at the mastery of visual accuracy, which, without the aid of any strict measuring, gives to every figure a grace which surpasses that of the merely regular. Its painting has succeeded in endowing the muscles of the limbs with that grace and gentle ease which lie between the seen and the unseen, displaying the vital ease of slender and graceful figures, especially women and children, as well as the limbs and joints of the male figure, created according to nature and clothed in the fullness of flesh, while not appearing gnarled as they often are in nature, but artistically ennobled by design and sensibility; furthermore, a wealth of beautiful draperies, a multitude of new and distinctive fancies, the subtlety of colour, all manner of painted architecture, and a variety of background landscape.

Vasari extols Leonardo da Vinci as the great initiator of the third period: 'With boldness and mastery of design . . . all in good style, admirable scheme and proportion, divinely graceful, this master, as rich in imitating the good as he was profound in his own artistic skill, succeeded indeed in endowing his figures with the motions and spirit of real life.' Other great artists who followed in this period were Perugino, Giorgione, and Fra Bartolommeo, though all were surpassed by 'the magnificent Raphael of Urbino, who studied the results of all the older and younger artists and possessed himself of the best of them all. . . . Nature itself had to yield before his colours, and those who see his historical pictures will find that in their lightness and objective inven‚ tion they stand equal to the written histories, depicting landscapes, buildings and people in our own country and abroad, in character and costume, as he wished to represent them.'

Others came later, Vasari says, but with more delicate colour and less vigour and attack in expression: Andrea del Sarto, who occupied a special position as an artist, 'for his works are faultless'; Antonio da Correggio, Francesco Mazzola (Parmigianino), and Sebastiano (del Piombo). In this class, Mannerist painter as he was, he also names Poli‚ doro (da Caravaggio), Giulio Romano, and Perino del Vaga. He especially praises the *facilità* of these painters. 'As for this art in general,' he says, 'these artists rendered it so perfect and facile for all who master design, invention and colour, that whereas formerly our artists finished one panel in six years, they can now complete six pictures in one year, as I can personally testify from my own observation and practical experience; moreover, these pictures are far better finished and more perfect than those others that earlier painters were able to produce.'

Vasari then comes to the coping‚stone of his structure:

> The master among all the living and the dead who bears the palm, who surpasses and excels all others in his glory, is the divine Michel‚ angelo Buonarroti, who holds the leadership not only in one art, but in all three together. . . . Thus from this fine and fruitful tree so many and such splendid branches now spread that they have won‚ drously filled the world with the most aromatic fruits, and have carried our three prized arts to their furthest limits of the most supreme and wonderful perfection.

Vasari's system seems at first sight fairly plausible, but his theory of evolution, purporting to show a steady progression through three periods of time, will not stand a closer analysis. It cannot rightly be regarded as the result of study, but rather as a premise and a postulate. In the *Lives* we find his record and judgment assuming a predominantly historical character. It gradually develops into a framework for his and the Renaissance view of the artists and their work, with a leaning towards the concrete and with relatively little emphasis on the theoretical and on consequent general conclusions.

In a later age artistic values are seen from a different angle. The 'first period' of painting, which Vasari considered beginnerish and awkward, possesses in fact, to the modern eye, a genuine 'primitive' quality of great attractiveness, a simplicity of expression, and an abstract departure from naturalism which raise the painters of this period far above 'awk-wardness'. In our opinion, Giotto and his pupils, as well as other artists of the Trecento, have greater vigour and vitality, and some, like Simone Martini and the Lorenzetti, more charm and feeling, than many extreme naturalistic painters of a later period. In reading Vasari, one suspects that he had his difficulties. As noted at various points in this book, he had to achieve a balance between his intuitive admiration of the primitives, notably Giotto, and his outwardly inspired opinion. The originality and concentration of Giotto in fact held a great appeal for him, but that master's greatness did not fit properly into his scheme. Vasari's dilemma is plain to see: he has no sooner expressed praise for the primitives than he is reminded of his readers, and especially of his fellow-artists, and feels himself obliged to retract and point out how far they still were from great painting.

While there is no denying that the fifteenth century made great advances through the employment of mathematics, the laws of per-spective, the study of anatomy, practical skill, and better technique, we can no longer agree that Vasari's second period marks a continuous scaling of the heights. In the intrinsic aspect of art – the relationship be-tween the psychology of the artist and the object in nature – we fail to see any development, any *increasing value*, as between the early masters of the century, like Masaccio, Mantegna and Castagno, and the later ones such as Gozzoli, Botticelli and Ghirlandaio.

If we turn to Vasari's third period, the sixteenth century, 'our own century', which is the period of Raphael and Michelangelo, though we can appreciate his enthusiasm for this culmination of art, we find, if we leave out Michelangelo as the timeless genius he was, that it is to no small extent the 'perfection', the virtuosity, the illusionist painting, which constitute Vasari's *summum bonum*. These are not qualities which we rate highest today – especially in the light of the contemporary non-Tuscan and non-Roman painters such as Giorgione, Titian and their school.

As a critic, Vasari is committed by the ideals of his time: the supreme development of painting in plastic-linear form as manifested in Michel-angelo and Raphael. He originally assesses all painters according to this standard, including those who must have had other and different quali-fications. It follows that he is not very responsive to the impulses towards a new and better style of painting that were felt by Leonardo and the Venetians, though with time his judgments become modified. He can-not disregard contemporary writers who are beginning to break away from the Florentine tradition, particularly Pietro Aretino, for whom he has great respect, and who writes of an 'ideal continuation' of Leo-nardo's ideas. Nor in the long run can his professional eye as a painter fail to be fascinated by what was new and emancipated.

Vasari gradually arrives at intuitive views which are contrary to his own fixed doctrine; he realizes that it is possible to achieve art not merely by imitating nature but also by absorbing the theory and style of other painters.

In the years between the first and second editions of the *Lives* the new ideas permeated his original opinions of Michelangelo and Raphael. In the works of Michelangelo he first sees only divine perfection, but later he makes reservations. 'Greatness in art', he says, 'is in one born of industry, in another of study, in this man of imitation, in that of scientific knowledge.' He sees that in addition to strictly plastic form there are other values, such as qualities and shades of colour, the importance of setting, landscape, space, and figures in the landscape.

In 1550 Vasari thinks that the art of Raphael reaches its real peak in those works where his imitation of Michelangelo is most apparent. In 1568 he believes that in this respect Raphael 'lost some of the good reputation he had gained'. He realizes now that Raphael best reveals

his own personality in those works which lie outside the style of Michelangelo, and which are characterized by lively invention, richness of
perspective and drapery, of beauty in the figures, and of portraiture.
'Raphael', he says, 'took note of these facts; and as he could not equal
Michelangelo in his nudes, he resolved to rival him and perhaps excel
him in these [other] fields.'

Here we get a glimpse of Vasari as a critic in the modern sense of that
term. Writing in another context, he says: 'Everyone should be content
to do those things to which he feels naturally attracted, instead of striving
to compete in what does not come naturally to him, and so struggling in
vain and reaping only shame and injury.'

The fact that Vasari's overall view of painting during the preceding
three hundred years cannot be endorsed and his evolutionary theory
must be disallowed, should not determine our appreciation of him as
an art historian. His theory was a working hypothesis, without which
– as he himself indicates – he would never have embarked on the bold
attempt, as it was then, to compile and clarify such a mass of material.
He brought to life for posterity an impressive array of artistic personalities; often he elucidated as well as possible their psychological and
somatic peculiarities, their character, industry, inclinations, and opinions,
spicing all this with traditional or personally experienced anecdotes,
whether true or (in some cases) doubtful. He strove honestly to docu-
ment the increasing ability of painters, and to judge their motives and
styles as he saw them. In a fair number of cases he saw individual new
creations acquire universal significance, and he was aware of the influence which certain localities and schools had on the trend of development. He wanted to interpret the lessons of the past for his colleagues,
enabling them by insight into historical continuity to possess and increase
the store of knowledge and ability that had been bequeathed to them.

Vasari has been criticized as a writer for not having achieved that
detached, aloof approach which exacting readers might have wished for.
It is true that in the sources he used for his account of the primitives, in
his own scattered comments on design, in his observations on works by

the primitives, the Quattrocento artists, Leonardo and the Venetians, even in the ideas of Mannerist critics, there is material which could have led him to an understanding of the 'aesthetic personality', whose creative power, as Lionello Venturi says, consists not only in individuality of character but also in the universal, the eternal, which is independent of rationality, current rules, and formulae. Such a concept was necessarily reserved for a later age. Vasari was bound by tradition, and his captivation by Michelangelo was a wall he could not penetrate.

Our own time, which can look back on a further three centuries of changing tastes and experimental schools of painting, so far-reaching that Vasari could never have dreamt of them, should be in a position to judge him with an unbiased eye. No more than we should today regard the books of Tycho Brahe and Kepler as expressing the last word on astronomy should we view Vasari's biographies and opinions on art in the light of the present day alone.

All those who are interested in the art of painting down the ages remain indebted to Vasari for his collection of material and the basis which it provides for discussion. His views and opinions, revealing the artistic aims of the Renaissance, have for centuries vitally influenced European ideas about art. What is more, his strong assertion of the High Renaissance in the art of Italian painting as the culmination of all time exerts through the *Lives* a powerful influence on wide circles to this day.

Chapter VII

'Accept my work in good part'

IN THE light of what has come down to us, it should now be possible to form a reliable picture of Vasari as a person. Portraits all represent him as a big man of considerable presence and strongly marked features, with a full beard (which he grew from the age of thirty), and a deep brow surmounting intelligent eyes which have a keen and confident gaze. His health was undoubtedly good throughout life, and his physique enabled him to travel incessantly on horseback on poor roads – doubtless extremely tiring in those days – and at all times to work incredibly hard. There is little evidence in his autobiography or anywhere else of illnesses or ailments; only of brief periods of indisposition due especially to overwork. The only occasion when he had to give up was during the period of his first stay in Rome. Excessive work, irregular eating habits and late hours, capped by an intense heatwave, forced him to lay down his brush and pencil and have himself carried home to Arezzo in a litter. For three or four months he lay ill at home with 'Roman fever', which seems to have been malaria, and which developed into *febris quartana*, or four-day fever.

Vasari must have possessed considerable equanimity, doubtless reinforced by a phlegmatic temperament. We find him travelling, painting, building, writing, and attending to his personal interests – his plans and the course of his work seeming to be little affected by the hardships and tribulations of his country.

The autobiography is concerned almost entirely with outward facts and has little to say about inner personal experiences which influence his mental development, about literary interests – apart from studies for 'the Book' – or about critical doubts and spiritual struggles. More traits which illustrate his outlook on life, with its hopes and disappointments, appear in the letters. While in correspondence from friends we find hints and insinuations about high living, we look in vain for indications of youthful romance, frivolity, or stories of love. His five-year 'courtship' does not suggest that affairs of the heart weighed heavily on his mind. There is nothing in the written sources which relate to any deeper approach to family life, domestic bliss, celebrations with friends, the pleasures of the table, playgoing, or other private or public entertainment.

Probably Vasari was unmusical; at any rate his references to music are scant and lack warmth. While he says that Leonardo, Giorgione, Titian, Sebastiano, Giulio Romano and Benvenuto Cellini were all masters in the handling of instruments, particularly the lute, we get never a tinkle from himself.

Nothing seems able to turn him from the path of industry and hard work and his – one is tempted to say – monomanic study and worship of art and artists.

It was Vasari's ambition to become a leader and an authority; in the first place he wished to equal in fame his ideal, Michelangelo, but he also wanted at all costs to achieve social position and wealth. His entire way of life had to be adapted to those ends. His path was charted in extreme youth. Of his thoughts at the age of twenty, when he visited Rome for the first time, he writes in his autobiography what we may read as a manifesto:

Moreover, I was deeply stimulated by a desire for fame, realizing that others ranked with the chosen and had achieved status and honour. Thus I would often say to myself: why is it not in my power to attain by continuous endeavour that greatness and position to which others have attained? Like myself, they are flesh and blood. Accordingly, driven by such deep and intense feelings – as well as by the demands of my family – I resolved that I should spare no toil, effort, late hours or other deprivations in order to achieve that goal. And with that aim in mind I never neglected either then or later, in Florence or anywhere else, to draw everything!

The theme of the poor but gifted artist who achieved honour and riches fascinated him, and in the *Lives* he returned to it again and again.

Vasari remained true to his intention throughout his life. With his practical flair, he early realized that his path must lead by way of the great – at the courts of the Popes and the Medici. He was a collector of distinctions, property and gold. His fees were some of the best of those days; beginning with twenty gold *scudi*, he had soon risen to 100, 200, 300, even 500 *scudi* or more a time. At the peak of his activities he received for his work on the Palazzo Vecchio, in addition to his regular salary, a sum of 1,200 *scudi* and a further one of 2,000 *scudi*. Vasari earned good money and was glad to do so, and yet he was by no means close-fisted. Besides devoting large sums to his own houses, the acquisition of works of art and antiquities, the fitting out of his chapel, and so forth, he spent substantial amounts on his many journeys, and he kept open house for his friends and clients. Whenever any of these called on him, as they frequently did when passing through, he would put them up for the night and entertain them regally.

Vasari's prosperity and general social status endowed him with real dignity and a deep-seated self-respect. He had no use for colleagues who lacked proper ambition and could not adjust themselves to civil ways. This view is vividly illustrated by his account of a mediocre painter, Iacone di Giovanni di Francesco, of Florence. A fellow-pupil under Andrea del Sarto, he had fallen to the level of leader of the city's Bohemians. He was fond of slandering and ridiculing Vasari, especially when the latter was out of town.

Iacone's head was always more full of horseplay than of study and work. He was one of a group who lived by their wits: I mean like pigs and cattle. They never washed their faces, their heads, or their beards; they never combed their hair and beards but once every other month; they used their cartoons for table-cloths; and they drank from the bottle or jug. They considered this life very fine – and were obviously as dirty in their minds as they were in their appearance. . . . Their main occupation was to gather in shops and other places and then spend their time in malicious gossip and in disparaging the works of decent men. . . . Iacone was the worst of them all!

One day, when Vasari was returning on horseback to the city, accompanied by a servant, Iacone, with a group of cronies, greeted him with one of his coarse remarks: 'Well, Giorgio, how are you doing?' 'Very well, my dear Iacone,' Giorgio replied. 'Once I was poor, like all of you, but now I have my three thousand *scudi* and more. . . . Once I served among you, but now I have a servant of my own to help me and look after my horse. Once I wore the clothes that poor painters wear, but now I have a velvet coat. Formerly I walked, but now I ride. So, my dear Iacone, *I* am doing very well. God speed you!'

Vasari says that hearing all this poor Iacone at once lost his tongue and was struck with amazement, realizing apparently the extent of his own wretchedness.

Fame also came to Vasari – if not always, or in every respect, as he deserved. With intuitive sureness he realized when young that he would have to imitate the greatest; and so he studied the work of Raphael and cultivated Michelangelo.

It can scarcely be affirmed that Vasari was a man of independent or unyielding character; or that idealism dominated his life and activities. Extremely compliant by nature, he had little difficulty in accommodating himself to circumstances. To his friends and patrons he was exceedingly willing and obliging, and he returned the benevolence of the Medici with a full heart, but nowadays we should most likely have called him a clever careerist and something of a snob.

In any consideration of Vasari's faults – as we see them – it is necessary to take account of the directness and coarseness of the times. Most of the 'best people' were grasping, selfish, sharp-tempered and vengeful. To all appearance, Vasari was highly respected and well liked. At the same time it is unthinkable that a man of his type could fail to give offence in various quarters. He occasionally met with a certain degree of coolness, especially from his collaborators. As I have mentioned, there was dissatisfaction among his assistants, master craftsmen as well as workmen, during the preparations for the entry into Florence of Charles v; in fact, they went on strike. During the work of building the Uffizi, when he made heavy demands on his staff, his foremen became disgruntled, complained to the Duke, and went so far as to impugn his personal integrity. They were flatly rebuffed by the Duke.

Vasari had at least one avowed enemy – Benvenuto Cellini. If we can take his word for it – which we should think twice about doing – Vasari was mean and petty. 'Giorgetto', as Benvenuto mockingly calls him in his colourful memoirs, was prone to scandal and created bad blood between him and the Duke, who was told unpleasant tales about him. 'This bad turn had been done to me by Giorgetto, a painter of Arezzo, perhaps to repay me for all the good turns I had done him. He had stayed with me in Rome at my expense, and had turned my house upside down. The fact is, he suffered from scab and was always scratching at it; and while sleeping in the same bed as my excellent assistant Manno, and meaning to scratch himself, had torn the skin off Manno's leg with those filthy claws of his, whose nails he never used to cut. Manno then left my service and would have made short work of him, had I not reconciled them. I then got Giorgio a position with Cardinal de' Medici (!), and always used to help him in one way or another, in gratitude for which he told Duke Alessandro that I had spoken ill of his Excellency, and that I had boasted I should be the first to scale the walls of Florence with his exiled enemies. . . .'

This account contradicts on essential points the one given by Vasari himself, and seems, to put it mildly, an exaggeration. Vasari was by nature considerably more careful and peace-loving than Benvenuto was. In no way did he deserve the lampoon which Benvenuto wrote about him and his friend Borghini, and which includes the lines:

> *Aretine Giorgio and the prior, that brother,*
> *While appearing as two are in fact one another. . . .*
> *What a tiresome couple, the prior of Nocente*
> *And that terrible cur, his fellow Giorgetto.*
> *For sure they have only been chosen by God*
> *To do here on earth all the havoc they could.*

Vasari was well aware that Benvenuto slandered him both to his friends and in the highest places, and that he easily took offence. When they sat together on the committee that had been appointed by the members of the Florentine Academy to make preparations for the funeral of Michelangelo, with Vasari as the chairman, a proposal put forward by Benvenuto for an elaboration of the catafalque was rejected, whereupon he withdrew from all further meetings of the committee.

In the *Lives* Vasari treats Benvenuto rather nonchalantly, but he did not leave him out, as Borghini had suggested that he should. Borghini wrote to him, 'It seems to me that you will disfigure this book of yours if you include among so many admirable men that swine Benvenuto.' The rather brief sketch closes with these words:

Although I could write at greater length on the work of Benvenuto, who in all his affairs has been biased, bad-tempered, excitable and abominable, and who unfortunately has had the habit of contributing by his lips no less than in art he has contributed by his hands, yet will I say no more than this: inasmuch as he has written of his own life and works, of the art of the goldsmith, of melting and casting metals and of other things associated with such arts, as well as of sculpture, with far greater eloquence than I could do, let this summary account of his very rare principal works suffice.

Vasari knew that Benvenuto had written his autobiography, but fortunately he did not read it, as it did not appear until after his death.

In spite of the revival of learning and the enthusiasm for culture, the age was callous and inhuman, especially in time of war and siege, which usually prevailed. The enforcement of the law was arbitrary; retribution, robbery and private revenge were rampant. The authority and reputation of the Church among the general population were tottering; all manner of worldliness and licentiousness reigned at the papal court, to the anger of ordinary citizens; the monastic system was becoming increasingly degenerate and was deservedly in disrepute.

At the same time gifted scholars and writers enjoyed a golden age because of the great desire for reading and knowledge, and because high fees were paid. Yet to our eyes even the most celebrated were corrupt. Historical and literary scholarship was not over-particular as regards objectivity, or pedantic in the matter of truth and untruth, or even plagiary.

Such opposites as Vasari's biographer-colleague, Paolo Giovio, the most distinguished man of letters of his day, and Benvenuto Cellini, its most conceited and garrulous memoirist, both lied – the one elegantly, the other grossly. Giovio, who specialized in eulogizing the great dead in highly fashionable and well-paid epitaphs, was liberal with his flattery, while at the same time he could be subtly malicious or sarcastic between the lines. Cellini, whose autobiography is brilliantly fresh, was extremely offensive and prejudiced where the reputation of others was concerned, and at the same time indecently boastful and self-glorifying. And what is one to say of Pietro Aretino, who combined great talent, considerable skill, high poetry and coarse humour with paid lampooning and undisguised blackmail?

All in all, Vasari seems to have been incomparably more honest than his colleagues, and his moral conduct gave little occasion for reproach. In fact it should surprise us that Vasari was able to accomplish his mission so honestly and openly as he did. The fuss which later writers on art have made of his 'shiftiness and shallowness' is misplaced and must seem to present-day readers, who can view his work in historical perspective, to be rather cheap. It is to be assumed that, having completed his preparations for the book, Vasari was overwhelmed by his material, which could only be raw material, and – in view of the brevity of life and his own meagre time – wanted at all cost to 'get it out', leaving others to embroider and correct it later.

Generally speaking, many of the faults that have been found in Vasari will at that time have passed for trifles, and give no occasion for hair-splitting now – inasmuch as no one can tell how much of what is written today will last. We can draw on his immense fund of material, arriving perhaps at different conclusions, but forming and supplementing impressions of the great artists, while using it as a basis for discussion of present-day problems in painting.

Vasari must have possessed extremely engaging qualities; originality of judgment and opinions worth listening to; attractiveness in company and conversation which led people of the highest standing to gather round him and seek his friendship. On the testimony of gifted contemporaries, he was a paragon of skill and integrity.

We can now see that Vasari's strength was an immense professional curiosity, sustained by technical knowledge and coupled with a delight in research and collecting. Even now we must marvel at his wide reading, his talent for interviewing, the pleasure he takes in narrating – all reflecting both his sense of the well-pointed anecdote and his genuine love of art and eagerness to celebrate it.

Vasari was a man of the Renaissance for good and ill, with a definite preponderance of the positive aspects of the concept: this man from whose work art lovers and art historians have drawn nourishment for four hundred years, and to whom ordinary readers have gone for his inexhaustible storehouse of art and period history, and for his lively, modern journalism. He created that pleasing combination of factual information and fascinating accounts of private life which spices historical biography today.

In dedicating the *Lives* to Duke Cosimo, Vasari says: '. . . It was not my purpose to win fresh fame as an author, but as an artist to praise the industry of art and preserve the memory of those who have laboured in this noble enterprise, and who therefore deserve that their names and works shall not in time to come be a prey to death and oblivion.'

For all his marked sense of his own worth, Vasari is alive to the importance of modesty in public conduct, as he expresses it at the end of the *Lives* when he addresses the 'Masters of Design': 'Let that be enough about myself, who now, after much labour, have reached the age of fifty-five and am ready to live for as long as it may please God, in His honour and in the service of my friends, and for the promotion and improvement of our noble art to the extent that my powers will permit. . . . Accept my work in good part, and do not expect of me what I do not know and cannot perform, being assured of my good intention, which is and always will be to give benefit and pleasure to others.'

Principal Italian editions

VASARI, GIORGIO: *Le vite de' più eccellenti Architetti, Pittori et Scultori Italiani, da Cimabue insino a' tempi nostri; descritte in Lingua Toscana da M. Giorgio Vasari Aretino; con una sua utile & necessaria Introduzione all' Arte Loro; In Fiorenza MDL* (1550).

Id.: *Le vite de' più eccellenti Pittori, Scultori et Architettori, Scritte & di nuovo Ampliate da M. Giorgio Vasari, Pittore et Architetto Aretino . . . con i Ritratti Loro et con l'aggiunta delle Vite de' vivi, & de' morti dall'anno 1550 insino al 1567. In Fiorenza, appresso i Giunti 1568.*

Id.: (ed. Carlo Manolessi, Bologna, 1647–8).

Id.: (ed. Giovanni Bottari, Rome, 1759–60).

Id.: (ed. Giovanni della Valle, Siena, 1791–8).

Id.: *Opere di Giorgio Vasari, Pittore Aretino* (ed. S. Audin, Florence, 1822–3).

Id.: (ed. F. Lemonnier and G. Milanesi, Florence, 1846–57).

Id.: (ed. Gaëtano Milanesi, Florence, 1878–85).

Id.: (ed. Pio Pecchiai, Milan, 1930–8).

Other editions

SCHORN, L., and E. FOERSTER: *Giorgio Vasari: Leben der ausgezeichnetsten Maler, Bildhauer und Architekten* . . . (Stuttgart and Tübingen, 1832–49).

FREY, KARL: *Ausgewählte Biografien aus Giorgio Vasari: Leben* . . . (Berlin, 1884–7).

GRONAU, G., A. GOTTSCHEWSKI and E. JAESCKE: *Giorgio Vasari: Die Lebensbeschreibungen der berühmtesten Architekten, Bildhauer und Maler* . . . (Strasbourg, 1904–10).

FREY, KARL: *Giorgio Vasari: Le Vite de' più eccellenti Pittori, Scultori ed Architetti* . . . (Munich, 1911). Only one volume published.

JEAURON and LECLENCHÉ: *Giorgio Vasari: La Vie des plus excellents Peintres, Sculpteurs et Architects* . . . (Paris, 1839–42).

FOSTER, J., and J. F. RICHTER: *Giorgio Vasari: Lives of the most Excellent Painters, Sculptors and Architects* . . . (London, 1885–7).

VERE, GASTON DE: *Vasari's Lives of the Most Eminent Painters, Sculptors and Architects* (London and New York, 1912–15).

HINDS, A. B.: *Vasari's Lives of the Painters, Sculptors and Architects* (London and New York, 1900).

BROWN, G. BALDWIN (ed.): *Vasari on Technique* (transl. Louisa E. Maclehose; London, 1907).

Vasari and his times

ADELMANN, G. S., and G. WEISS: *Das Fortleben gotischer Ausdrucks- und Bewegungsmotive in der Kunst des Manierismus* (Tübingen, 1954).

BERENSON, BERNARD: *The Italian Painters of the Renaissance* (London, 1952).

BRIGANTI, GIULIO: *Il Manierismo e Pellegrino Tibaldi* (Rome, 1945).

Id.: *Italian Mannerism* (London, 1963).

BURCKHARDT, J.: *The Civilization of the Renaissance in Italy* (London, 1951).

CARDEN, R. W.: *The Life of Giorgio Vasari* (London, 1910).

CELLINI, BENVENUTO: (Various English editions).

CONDIVI, ASCANIO: *The Life of Michael Angelo Buonarroti* (London, 1911).

DVOŘÁK, M.: *Geschichte der italienischen Kunst II* (Munich, 1928).

FREY, K. and H-W.: *Der litterarische Nachlass Giorgio Vasaris I–II. Ricordanze di Giorgio Vasari* (Munich, 1923 and 1940).

Id.: *Neue Briefe* (Burg, 1940).

GREGOROVIUS, F.: *History of the City of Rome in the Middle Ages* (8 vols., London, 1900–9).

KALLAB, WOLFGANG: *Vasaristudien*. Vol. 15 of *Quellenschriften für Kunstgeschichte und Kunsttechnik des Mittelalters* (Vienna and Leipzig, 1908).

MOTTINI, G. E.: *Storia dell' Arte Italiana* (Milan, 1949).

OLSEN, HARALD: *Federico Barocci: a critical study in Italian Cinquecento Painting* (Uppsala, 1962).

PAATZ, WALTER: *Die Kunst der Renaissance in Italien* (Stuttgart, 1953).

PACCAGNINI, G.: *La Peinture Italienne* (Geneva and Paris, 1953).

SCHLOSSER, J. von: *La letteratura artistica* (ed. O. Kurze; Vienna and Florence, 1956).

VENTURI, ADOLFO: *Storia dell'Arte Italiana I–XI* (Milan, 1901–40).

VENTURI, LIONELLO: *History of Art Criticism* (New York, 1936).

Id.: *Painting and Painters* (New York and London, 1946).

VITA, ALESSANDRO del (ed.): *Il Vasari, Rivista d'Arte e di Studi vasariani* (Arezzo, 1927–43 and 1957–). This includes *Il libro delle Ricordanze di Giorgio Vasari; Inventario e Regesto dei Manoscritti dell'Archivio Vasariano; lo Zibaldone di Giorgio Vasari; il Carteggio di Giorgio Vasari.*
All these are also published separately by Reale Istituto d'Archeologia e Storia dell'Arte (Rome and Arezzo, 1938–41).

VOSS, HERMANN: *Die Malerei der Spätrenaissance in Rom und Florenz I–II* (Berlin, 1920).

WITTKOWER, RUDOLF: *Art and Architecture in Italy 1600–1750* (Pelican History of Art series; London and New York, 1958).

Index

Page numbers in italics refer to illustrations

Accademia del Disegno, Florence (founded 1563), 64, 141

Accademia della Virtù, Rome (founded 1530), 31

Alberti, Leon Battista (architect, 1404–72), 86, 132

Alessandro de' Medici, Duke of Florence (1510–37), 27, 29, 33, 40–1

Altoviti, Bindo (banker, b. 1491), 43, 47, 51, 87

Ammannati, Bartolomeo (architect and sculptor, 1511–92), 60, 64, 73, 87

Andrea del Castagno (painter, 1390–1457), *103*, 133, 155–6, 162

Andrea del Sarto (d'Agnolo; painter, 1486–1531), 29, 54, 72, 85, *111*, 112, *135*, *148*, 154, 161

Angelico, Fra (Fra Giovanni da Fiesole; painter, 1387–1455), 25, 94, *101*, *108*

Archivio Vasari, 10, 14, 85

Aretino, Pietro (essayist and dramatist, 1492–1556), 43, 44–5, *48*, 49, 120, 143, 156, 163, 172

Arezzo, *18*, 25, 58

Ariosto, Ludovico (poet, 1474–1533), 129

Arnolfo di Lapo di Cambio (architect, 1240–1311), 60

Averlino, Antonio (Filarete; architect, sculptor and writer, c. 1400–69), 132, 153

Bacci, Francesco, Vasari's father-in-law, 53

Badia di Arezzo, 55, 59, 75

Bandinelli, Baccio (sculptor and painter, 1493–1560), 29, 76

Barocci, Federico (Fiori; painter, 1528–1612), 80

Barozzi, Iacopo (Vignola; architect, 1507–73), 73

Bartoli, Cosimo (theologian), 142

Bellini, Gentile (painter, 1429–1507), 110

Bellini, Giovanni (painter, 1430–1516), 110, *115*, *146*

Bellini, Iacopo (painter, c. 1400–70), 109–10

Berenson, Bernard, 81

Bibbiena, Cardinal Bernardo (1470–1520), 31, 115

Boccaccio, Giovanni (poet, 1313–75), 129, 141

Borghini, Vincenzo (vice-president, Accademia del Disegno, 1515–80), 19, *48*, 53, 141–2, 151, 156, 171

Bottari, Giovanni, 21, 22

Botticelli, Sandro (Alessandro Filipepi; painter, 1444–1510), 94, 109, *113*, *118*, 162

Bramante, Donato (architect and painter, 1444–1514), 86–7

Bronzino, Angelo (Tori; painter, 1502–72), 34, 37–8, 64, 84

Brunelleschi, Filippo (architect, 1377–1446), 86, 133

Burckhardt, Jacob (art historian, 1818–97), 134

Cancelleria, La, 51–3, *66*, 67, 72, 87

Caro, Annibale (writer, 1507–66), 19, 72, 97

Carrucci, Iacopo (Pontormo; painter, 1494–1557), 33, 34, 37, 38, *46*, 80, 81, 84, *113*, *135*

Carteggio di Giorgio Vasari, Il, 137–8

Casa Vasari, Arezzo, *35*, 58, 137

Cellini, Benvenuto (sculptor and goldsmith, 1500–72), *48*, 71, 151, 167, 170–1

Cennino di Drea Cennini (painter and writer, b. 1372), 130, 157

Cesano, Gabriello (lawyer, b. *c.* 1500), 40

Charles V, Emperor (1500–58), 30, 38, *68*

Chigi, Agostino (financier, 1465–1520), 114, 119

Cimabue, Giovanni (dei Pepi; painter, 1241–1303), 22, *39*, 77, 91, 130

Cinquecento, 162–3

Clement VII, Pope (Giulio de' Medici), 33, 40, 41, 47, *68*, 154

Compagnia et Fraternità di S. Luca, Florence, 64

Condivi, Ascanio (painter and writer, *c.* 1520–74), 133

Cornell, Henrik (art historian), 81

Correggio, Antonio (Allegri; painter, *c.* 1494–1534), 43–4, *146*, 161

Cosimo de' Medici the Elder (1389–1464), 33, 102

Cosimo de' Medici the Younger, Grand Duke of Tuscany (1519–74), 19, 39–40, 41, 42, *46*, 56–7, 59, 60–2, 69, 138–41, 173

Cosina (Nicolosa di Francesco Bacci), Vasari's wife, 45, *46*, 53–7, 64, 69

Cristofano Coriolano (Venetian woodengraver), 20

Dante Alighieri (poet, 1265–1321), 129, 130

Doceno, Cristofano, *see* Gherardi, Cristofano

Doni, Paolo di (Uccello; painter, 1397–1475), 25, 94, 132

Duccio (Bernarduccio?) di Buoninsegna (painter, *c.* 1250–1318), 91, 92, *105*

Duecento, 90, 157

Dürer, Albrecht (painter, 1471–1528), 34, 37, 114

Eleonora di Toledo, Grand Duchess of Tuscany (d. 1562), 60

Farnese, Cardinal Alessandro (1520–89), 15, 47, 51–2, 116, 149

Filarete, Antonio, *see* Averlino, Antonio

Filippino Lippi (painter, 1457–1504), 104

Filippo Lippi (painter, 1406–69), 101–4, *108*

Flemish painters, 128

Francesca, Piero della (painter, 1416–92), 23, 25, 94, 99–100, *117*, 132, 152

Francesco de' Medici, Hereditary Grand Duke of Tuscany (1541–87), 22
Fraternità dei Laici, Arezzo, 69, 75, 137
Frey, Hermann-Walther, 137
Frey, Karl, 137

Gherardi, Cristofano (Doceno; painter, 1508–56), 38–40, 50, 51
Ghiberti, Lorenzo (sculptor and bronze caster, 1378–1455), 72, 131, 133, 153
Ghirlandaio, Domenico (Bigardi; painter, 1449–94), 122, 162
Giorgione da Castelfranco (Giorgio Zorzi; painter, 1478–1510), 76, 84, 110–11, *123*, *147*, 160, 163, 167
Giottino (Giotto di Maestro Stefano; painter, 1324–70), 92, 130
Giotto di Bondone (painter and architect, 1266–1337), *39*, 91, *96*, *106*, 130, 158–9, 162
Giovio, Paolo (Paulus Iovius; bishop, physician and writer, 1483–1552), 15–16, 31, 43, *48*, 54, 139, 149–50, 156, 172
Giunti, Iacopo and Filippo (Florentine printers and publishers), 20
Gozzoli, Benozzo (painter, 1420– *c.* 1499), 162
Greco, El (Domenico Theotocopulos; painter, *c.* 1547–1614), 84
Gregorovius, F., 29, 49
Gregory XIII, Pope, 64
Guglielmo da Marcilla (Guillaume de Marseille; painter, d. 1529), 26

Ippolito de' Medici, Cardinal (1511– 35), 27, 30, 31, 40, 41, *47*
Istituto di Belle Arti, 64

Julius III, Pope, 53, 72

Lampsonius, Dominicus (Flemish humanist, b. *c.* 1532), 128
Leonardo da Vinci (painter, engineer and writer, 1452–1519), 84, 85, 97–8, *115*, 132–3, *145*, 160
Leoni, Francesco (banker), 44
Lives of the Most Excellent Painters etc., 12–13, *17*, 59, 85
planning and publication of, 15*ff.*
contents of, 89*ff.*
sources, 129*ff.*
Lombard, Lambert (Flemish painter and writer, 1505–66), 128
Lorenzetti, Ambrogio (painter, *c.* 1300– 48), *93*, *106*, 162
Lorenzetti, Pietro (painter, d. 1348), 25, 92, *105*, 162
Lorenzino de' Medici, murderer of Alessandro (1514–48), 41
Lorenzo de' Medici, 'The Magnificent' (1449–92), 33, *65*, 72
Luciani, Sebastiano, *see* Piombo, del
Lucrezia del Fede, wife of Andrea del Sarto, *148*, 154–5
Lucrezia di Francesco Buti, wife of Filippo Lippi, 104

Mannerism, 12, 37, 79*ff.*, 116
Manolessi, Carlo, 21, 22
Mantegna, Andrea (painter, 1431–1506), 98–9, *117*, 162
Martini, Simone (painter, 1285–1344), 77, 92, *93*, 130, 162
Masaccio (Tomaso di Ser Guidi; painter, 1401–28), 25, 85, 93–4, *99*, *107*, 159–60, 162

Michelangelo Buonarroti (painter, sculptor and architect, 1475–1564), 25, 28–9, 31, 51, 52, 61, 72, 83, 86–7, 89, 94, 114, 116, 119, 121*ff.*, 141–2, *145*, 161, 163

Michele Sanmicheli (architect and painter, 1488–1559), 51, 87

Michelozzo Michelozzi (architect, 1396–1472), 86

Milanesi, Gaetano, 21, 137, 152

Molza, Francesco Maria (humanist writer, 1489–1544), 19

Monte, Cardinal Giovanni del, *see* Julius III

Mottini, G. E., 80

Nicolosa di Francesco Bacci, *see* Cosina

Orange, Prince of (Filibert, Count of Chalons, *c.* 1499–1529), 29

Orcagna, Andrea (Cione; painter, *fl.* 1343–68), 92

Ottaviano de' Medici (d. 1546), 33, 42, 50

Palazzo alle Colonne, Arezzo, *18*, 75

Palazzo dei Cavalieri di S. Stefano, Pisa, 73–4, *95*

Palazzo dell' Orologio, Pisa, 74

Palazzo Farnese, Rome, 51, 87

Palazzo Vecchio, Florence, 60*ff.*, *67*, *68*, 71, 149

Palladio, Andrea (architect, 1508–80), 87

Parmigianino, Francesco (Mazzola; painter, 1503–46), 84, 161

Passerini, Cardinal Silvio, 27, 129

Paul III, Pope (Alessandro Farnese the Elder), 16, 52–3, *67*

Paulsson, Gregor, 53, 82

Pecchiai, Pio, 21, 137

Perugino, Pietro (Vannucci; painter, 1446–1523), 160

Peruzzi, Baldassare (architect and painter, 1481–1537), 31, 86

Petrarca, Francesco (poet and humanist, 1304–74), 25, 129

Piero della Francesca, *see* Francesca

Pieve di Arezzo, 69

Piombo, Sebastiano del (Luciani; painter and architect, 1485–1547), 47, 84, 119–120, *123*, *148*, 153–4, 161, 167

Pippi, Giulio, *see* Romano

Pitti, Don Miniato (abbot and writer, *c.* 1508–*c.* 1563), 19, 30, 42, 149, 156

Pius IV, Pope, 55

Pius V, Pope, 63, 142

Poggi, Giovanni, 137

Pollastra, Giovanni (Lappoli; poet), 26, 42

Ponte di Santa Trinità, Florence, 60

Pontormo, Iacopo, *see* Carrucci

Primitives, the, 91, 130, 162

Quattrocento, 84, 86, 93, 94, 98, 157, 165

Raffaello Sanzio, *see* Raphael

Ragionamenti sopra le Invenzioni etc., 22–3, 85

Raphael (painter and architect, 1483–1520), 43, 47, 94, *111*, 112–16, 133, *136*

Rasponi-Spinelli, Luciano, Count, 137
Robusti, Iacopo, *see* Tintoretto
Romano, Giulio (Pippi; painter and architect, 1499–1546), 43, 80, 81, 84, 115–16
Rosso Fiorentino (Giovanni Battista de' Rossi; painter, 1494–1541), 30, 31, 80, 84

Sachetti, Francesco (poet, *c.* 1330–*c.* 1400), 130
Sack of Rome, the, 31
Salviati, Francesco (de' Rossi; painter, 1510–63), 28, 32, 84, 153
Sangaletti, Guglielmo (Papal Secretary), 142
Sangallo, Antonio da, the elder (Giamberti; architect and painter, 1455–1534), 86
Sangallo, Antonio da, the younger (Giamberti; architect and painter, 1485–1546), 51
Sangallo, Giuliano (Giamberti; architect, 1445–1516), 86
Sansovino, Iacopo (Tatti; architect and sculptor, 1486–1570), 31, 44, 64, 87
Santo Stefano, Order of, 63, 73–4, 95
Santa Croce Church, Florence, 74–5
Signorelli, Luca (painter, *c.* 1441–1523), 25, 26, 100, *103, 118*

Tasso, Giambattista (wood-carver and architect, *c.* 1500–1552), 60–1
Tintoretto, Iacopo (painter, 1518–94), 64, 84, 111–12
Titian (Tiziano Vecellio da Cadore; painter, 1477–1576), 47, *48,* 64, 76, 84, 116, 119, *121, 147,* 163, 167

Tolomei, Claudio (writer, *c.* 1483–1555), 31
Torrentino, Lorenzo (printer and publisher), 19
Traini, Francesco (painter, *fl.* 1321–44), 92
Trecento, 84, 157, 162

Uccello, Paolo, *see* Dono
Uffizi Gallery, Florence, 16, 62, 75, *78,* 140, 170

Vaga, Perino del (painter and architect, 1499–1540), 80, 81, 161
Valeriano, Piero (humanist and writer), 28
Vasari, Giorgio (1511–74), *frontis.,* 46
and Mannerism, 79*ff.*
as architect, 59*ff.,* 63–4, 72*ff., 78,* 87–8
as painter, 36–7, 45, 46–7, *48,* 54, 55–7, 64, 65–8, 69, 71–2, 84
as writer, 151*ff.*
letters, 123, 126, 134*ff.*
Lives, see Lives
Vasari, Antonio (father), 25, 26, 29, 45, 140
Vasari, Don Antonio (uncle), 26, 29, 40
Vasari, Francesco Maria, 69, 137
Vasari, Giorgio (grandfather), 25–6, 45
Vasari, Lazzaro (great-grandfather), 25, 45, 140, 152
Vasari, Maddalena (mother), 25, 45, 140
Veneziano, Domenico (painter, *c.* 1400–61), 155–6
Venice, 44, 49
Venturi, Adolfo, 80–1, 89, 134, 151
Venturi, Lionello, 165

Vespucci, Nicolo, 27
Vignola, Iacopo, *see* Barozzi
Villa Giulia, Rome, 73, 95
Villani, Giovanni (historian, *c.* 1280–1348), 130, 131, 157
Vita, Alessandro del, 14, 137–8
Vite etc., *see Lives*

Vitruvius Pollio (architect, 1st century AD), 129
Voss, Hermann, 80

Zuccari, Federico (painter and writer, 1542–1609), 21–2, 69, 79, 85